Soccer Training
An Annual Programme

Note on usage: For better readability we decided on using the masculine (=neutral) language throughout this book. The feminime language is intended to be inclusive, of course.

Jozef Sneyers

SOCCER TRAINING

AN ANNUAL PROGRAMME

Meyer & Meyer Sport

Original title: Voetbal Trainingsboek
© Elmar Sport Rijswijk, Niederlande, 1985
Translated from the German edition by Paul D. Chilvers-Grierson

British Library Cataloguing in Publication Data
A catalogue for this book is available from the British Library

Sneyers, Jozef:
Soccer Training - An Annual Programm
- Oxford: Meyer und Meyer, (UK) ltd., 2002
ISBN 1-84126-017-7

© 2002 by Meyer & Meyer Sport (UK) Ltd.
Aachen, Adelaide, Auckland, Budapest, Graz, Johannesburg,
Miami, Olten (CH), Oxford, Singapore, Toronto
Member of the World

Sports Publishers' Association
www.w-s-p-a.org

Printed and bound in Germany
by Druckpunkt Offset GmbH, Bergheim
ISBN 1-84126-017-7
E-Mail: verlag@meyer-meyer-sports.com
www.meyer-meyer-sports.com

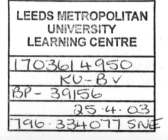

CONTENTS

CONTENTS

1 Foreword

This book is designed for all (youth) soccer coaches and for those directly involved in soccer training in other ways. It is based on the assumption that in youth teams the emphasis is more on precision and technique and less on great physical load. The focus is neither on theoretical discussions nor on high-faluting objectives. The objective is to develop a complete annual programme for a team in which all aspects of a soccer season are covered. We are assuming two training sessions a week. Each training session is described in full. In addition we directly follow the performance development of the team with regard to training preparation. Because improvisation is the best way of driving a team to desperation within the shortest time, and in order to avoid that we as coaches ourselves no longer know how to carry on after two weeks, the following questions must be answered:

* What players are available (strengths and weaknesses)?
* What can the coach develop in the way of game-tactical options taking into consideration the level and the composition of the team?

Answering these questions creates the foundation for the structure of an annual programme and from this the topics can be extrapolated, spread over the various periods, which must be covered during training. Of course our own personal understanding of the game also plays a role. This book thus only provides a guideline for various situations so that every coach is placed in a position to create his own programme using many examples and diagrams.

Two general comments in closing. Firstly: Ensuring variety in training does not mean that many different types of materials and different types of exercises must be involved. Quite the opposite is true, simple training flows much more freely. Secondly: There is a widespread but incorrect belief that training is only good when it "hurts" the players. The result is only that they walk around with sore muscles for days afterwards. If this happens frequently we can be sure that after a while fitness crises and injuries occur. To prevent this we must keep to a well thought out programme in which the preparatory period plays an important role. Only in the following championship period is it important that the available potential is expanded as effectively as possible, maintained and used. After all, the strength must be enough for a whole season.

2 Practical Soccer Training

Soccer is a team sport. Its foundations are technique, handling the ball and game understanding of the individual players. Furthermore a high degree of teamwork is expected of the players. All of these elements play an important role. The principle of soccer is simple, shoot goals and prevent the opponent from shooting goals. Whoever shoots the most goals has won. If we look at this extremely simplified objective, then we can see the following: In order to shoot a goal, the team must be in possession of the ball; in order to prevent the opponent from shooting a goal, it must attempt to turn a ball lost into ball possession. When we are in possession of the ball, we must, however, first develop goal opportunities and these must then be used. So we have to attack. If we lose the ball, we must try with all available means to prevent an opponent's goal and get back into possession. This means we must defend. How we solve these various tasks collectively within the team must be practised with the players during training. From a theoretical point of view, this is addressed during team meetings and in preparing for training.

It is essential that a coach gets to know his group of players as quickly as possible. He keeps his information (data) on a player file in order to maintain a total overview. At the end of this chapter we will show an example of such a player filing card. Of course this can be adapted to the particular wishes and experience of every coach. Just as necessary as getting to know one's own player group is knowing the opponent in each case. Every season you meet each opponent twice. It is therefore advisable to have a filing card on each opponent. The more data, the better. Try to collect up-to-date information on the most important opposing players by watching games of the opposing team. In any case, experience from the previous season cannot be the only thing to go by.

Training is not an end in itself. It is a means to prepare the eleven to play for points so that the players go onto the field in the best possible condition - physically, mentally and tactically. When structuring training the game must therefore be in one's mind. The focus is on the ball. Combination and speed ability exercises, increasing the speed of action as well as exercises related to game tactics must be trained again and again. In training the teamwork of the players must be developed so that after a while certain movements and movement patterns can be executed practically automatically. Fitness, speed ability, acceleration speed and of course the basic techniques are indispensable here. In addition, during the whole season we will place great value on playing without the ball; choosing positions, offering oneself, mutual covering etc. Playing without the ball is a tactical element. We will also have to explain the various roles which an individual player can take on in the course of a game. In this way the tactical instructions which are given to players for the game can be better understood and executed.

Another job of the coach is to create lasting motivation amongst the players. The best way to do this is with appropriate exercises with and without the ball. "Running laps" is of course not good. The players should experience and accept training, not put up with it. We must make sure that training does not run down between the individual exercises. Active relaxation exercises have their place here. The coach should always have the objective of the exercises in mind.

Examples:

1. In an exercise we place the emphasis on accuracy. In other words the objective is the exact execution of a movement or a game move. Certainly at the beginning the pace will be slow. Only when the execution is satisfactory will the speed (gradually) be increased.

2. We place the emphasis on speed. The greater the speed, the more difficult it is to fulfil the demand for accuracy. In practice it can be seen clearly when the maximum speed and the minimum accuracy necessary for an action to be successful intercept. This point can be shifted by working on the basic techniques of the players. A lapsing of the players or the wrong execution of tasks must be recognised in time and corrected without interrupting the rhythm of the exercise. On the other hand we must not forget to praise the players from time to time, without exaggeration of course.

Praise stimulates the players. One more thing in closing: if a player has not understood an exercise it is probably his own fault. If several players or even the whole group do not understand the exercise, it is highly likely to be the coach's fault. The causes are inaccurate explanations, insufficient explanations or the whole exercise may be illogical. In any case you must never forget: The coach knows the exercises theoretically and practically, for the player, however, everything is new.

Player filing card

Player's name: ....
Date of birth: ....
Home town: ....
Limited to ... years/unlimited * ....
Usually plays in the following position: ....
Most likes being positioned as: ....

Strong or less strong aspects:

1. Ball Technique: ....
2. Heading: ....
3. Speed Ability: ....
4. Goal shot: ....
5. Positional play: ....
6. Game division/game overview: ....
7. Supporting team mates: ....
8. Moving back when the ball is lost (defending): ....
9. Dealing with team mates: ....
10. Criticism and readiness for self criticism: ....
11. Physical: ....

Other characteristics:

Attitude: Offensive/Defensive * ....
Character: ....
Notes: ....

* delete not applicable

Information file on opposing teams

Club: ....
Date of games: ....
Results: ....
Formation (including changes): ....
Way of playing (various tactics): ....
Data of individual players: ....
Which tactics must we pursue? ....

3 Training Structure

Every coach knows that improvisation in training is bad. Training must be structured systematically. Corresponding to the kind of training, the emphasis is on a certain aspect. Training should be as follows:

1. Preparation of the players for training

Get the players to be in the changing room a quarter of an hour before starting. While changing, we briefly discuss what we are going to do and why. Prevent players from shooting at goal before the warm-up already (injuries).

2. Warm-up

Warming up and loosening the muscles as preparation for the main part. Duration and intensity according to the intention of training.

3. Main part of the training session

- *Fitness training:* improve and maintain physical condition
- *Technical exercises:* ball security (basis) and playing technique
- *Tactical exercises:* player groups, first, second and third row, significance of the front line, support during a tackle or defence, midfield, attack from the second row, offside traps etc.

4. Recovery

Training finishes with a series of unwinding exercises. The players must never go back to the changing rooms directly after the last exertions, but should come to rest while still outside by e.g. collecting the materials used. Only when the heart rate is back under 100 beats/min should they go to the changing rooms and have a shower. The content of the training session depends on the planned annual programme and the players' possibilities. The coach should not  do too much at once. Some difficult topics can only be learned gradually. Other subjects should be left out because they are not needed (training time is also valuable). The time within the season also plays a role. There is e.g. little point in beginning strength training at the end of the season.

Useful tips

- The players must be in a rested state for training and competition. Insist for example that they do not go to bed too late.
- Two hours before training or a competition players must not eat any more.
- Make sure there is sufficient space in the changing rooms and hot water (showers are a necessity).
- The greater the load in training, the longer and more intensive the warm-up phase must be (especially in fitness training).
- Don't let the players stand around too long in training, e.g. when something is being explained, especially not in cold weather, wind or after load. It is better if the players move around easily while you are explaining something.
- Do not carry out exercises while sitting or lying when the ground is damp or cold.
- If one or more of the players lose interest in training, try to find out the reasons (position in the team, sitting on the reserve bench, false nutrition, private or other difficulties, physical condition, attitude of other players, problems with club management, training itself).

Every training session must be well prepared methodologically:

1. *Prepare for the individual exercises.*
- Determine the objective.
- What do I want to teaching the players? (How do I achieve this objective?)
- How will I teach the players?
- Divide the exercise into phases (Analysis and synthesis of a game movement).
- Why will I teach this?
2. *Use the analysis sheets of the players and the player filing cards.*
3. *Make sure that everything is ready from the beginning.*
The necessary material must be available in sufficient quantities.
4. *Make sure that the training area is in order, exactly as you would expect it of the players.*
5. *After training, check whether the training objective set has been achieved.*

Take the following conclusions to heart for your training execution:

1. *Get your players in the right mood.*
- Make sure the players feel good.
- Tell them the aim of the exercise.
- Find out what the players already know about the exercises.
- Arouse their interest in the exercise.
- Show them a game phase which is related to the exercise.

2. *Show the exercise to the players.*
- Explain and show them the exercise phase for phase.
- Emphasise the main elements.
- Explain clearly, completely and patiently.
- Never do more than the players can take in at one time.

3. *Check the players.*
- Get them to execute the exercise and improve the mistakes.
- Make clear why.
- Keep going until the players have understood the exercise and execute it properly.

4. *Observe the players in practice.*
- Get them to execute a practised technique or tactical element in a training game.
- Have them play practice games with certain requirements or restrictions.

5. *After training find out how the players found it.*
Always be open for questions and encourage the players.

4 Factors which Affect Training

Experience shows that a well organised training positively influences results which gives the coach the necessary trust on the part of the players. If, however, there are no positive results or other problems arise, there is generally only one decision possible for those who have a say in the matter: change the coach. To put it simply: when signing his contract, the coach is already signing his own dismissal. The coach has a rather lonesome position.

No matter how well training is prepared and how strong the game shown is tactically in the points games: judgement of him will always depend on the bullseye. For this reason from the first moment on the coach must get to work with all his energy and observe all influencing factors. The prerequisite for a good training programme is that the coach expend his knowledge by evaluating technical literature, talking with other coaches, taking training courses, observing current developments in soccer etc.

With regard to equipment as well, the coach must leave nothing to chance. He must always have sufficient balls, cones, corner flags, hurdles, training vests etc. In addition he must make sure the changing rooms are kept tidy and that there is a blackboard for talks on technique and tactics. In general he must come to agreement with everybody who influences the success of his activity (players, family, fans, administration and staff), so that he can do his work in the best way possible and his players can go on to the competition field as well prepared as possible. The results of the training and coaching of a group of players are dependent on many factors.

1. Coach:

- Knowledge and training experience
- Character
- Views on the game
- Ability to motivate players.

2. Players:

- Existing qualities
- Training discipline
- Attitude to sport outside training time (use/abuse of alcohol, smoking, regulated life)

- Willingness to train independently outside of training to eliminate weak points
- Communal feeling and team spirit (gatherings, contacts amongst each other, other interests).

3. Environment:
Favourable or unfavourable influences can come from the club management, fans, the players' parents and, not to be forgotten, their wives or girlfriends.

5 Basic Techniques

Mastery of basic techniques determines the playing "substance" of a team. Tactics without technique are impossible, unless the tactics consist only of keeping one's own goal closed by "nailing it" and as far as possible shooting away every ball. Very few players will get enjoyment out of this. On the other hand, the better each individual player can handle the ball and the more prudently he acts in a game situation, the more successfully the team's game will run. We are assuming, however, that the players place their abilities at the service of the team. Soccer can be reduced to two situations: ball possession and loss of the ball. If the players master the basic techniques, they will stay in possession of the ball longer. The chance of positively shaping a game and converting ball possession into goal opportunities is thus greater. A team which demonstrates weaknesses in ball technique will more often be confronted with the situation of loss of the ball. The players will then hear from their coach how it should be, but they cannot put the theory into practice. In other words: tactical intentions and teamwork of the players can only be successfully realised if the basic techniques are mastered. The learning and training of basic techniques is a necessity. For this reason we will also ensure sufficient time for this during training. Handling the ball is a question of feeling for the ball and this can only be developed through frequent practice. Here are a number of elementary techniques which will appear in training: ball stopping and controlling with the foot, thigh, chest and head, rapid passing on of the ball, direct play, dribbling, attacking, moving with the ball,

short and long pass, sliding in, barging, throwing in the ball, direct and indirect free-kicks, short and long corners, headers, varying ways of putting a spin on the ball etc.

As coach we assume that none of the players with whom we are working is a blank sheet of paper. On the other hand we make sure that youth players are trained solidly in these elementary techniques. In both cases there are certain basic rules:

- We have players practise a movement sequence as long as it takes for this to be completely correctly executed from a technical point of view.
- Every incorrect handling of the ball is improved immediately.
- We teach the material as interestingly as possible (different formation, changed situations). The movement sequence (the training material) is repeated often, but each time in a different form (principle of varied practising).
- The practising of a particular game movement is always finished in a game-typical way. A game action of course never occurs in isolation. Example: after stopping and controlling the ball there is a pass or a shot at goal.

6 Expectations Placed on Coaches

In the end only one thing is expected of a coach: successes. How these successes are achieved is not important to most officials and fans. Neither is whether or not the coach has the right players for it. We have already pointed out that a coach who improvises his training will hardly have any successes. Good preparation is the first prerequisite. I myself prepare my training in two variations: one for normal situations and one for bad weather. In this respect I thus never have surprises. The structure of the training session must be worked out in detail beforehand. In peace and quiet those exercises are selected which are most suitable for the particular purpose. Because the execution has been determined beforehand, the training will be carried out briskly. The coach can increase the degree of difficulty or add another fitness aspect or do both. If this occurs gradually, players can better follow the various variations of execution. Well organised training also has the advantage that it becomes clear it is the work of an expert. For the players another reason to trust you, which will aid later work. Before the training period begins, the coach establishes an **annual programme.** In this he considers all data of significance for the individual training sections. He should divide up the annual programme into five periods:

Pre-season:
1. Preparatory period
2. Build-up period

High season:
3. Soccer-specific training
4. Points game training

Post-season (phase of regeneration and preparation for the new season)
The objective which the coach sets with a certain team and the requirements which result from the particular period for training determine how the various training elements are worked out. It goes without saying that the game experience of the season is taken into consideration. The various training elements then only need to be put into practical exercise forms. A coach who proceeds in this way will have an overview of the general training advances and be in a position to eliminate individual weaknesses of players as well as of the team

as a whole. Of course those things receive attention which are among the strong aspects during training. Their level must be kept up. To make the best use of competitive games the coach works with an analysis sheet with the aid of which he evaluates the points games. In doing so he can in some cases be assisted by a board member. The most important points - both the strong as well as the weak - which are observed in the game analysis are discussed with the players. Those issues which must have consequences for training can be incorporated into the training material without the coach having to vary too much from his (annual) programme. As this is a practical book, here is a practical example.

Example

In some preparatory games it becomes obvious that the midfield players are neglecting to play across the wings. It would be completely wrong to raise one's voice and announce during the game or shortly after it: "Folks, that's not on, you can't do it like that." The players must be made aware of these observations in a constructive way and afterwards go through them as training material.

The training material should not be given to them without explanation. If we were to begin with the exercises immediately, the result would be negative. The players would give their best, but get no further than an over-hasty game with bad passes. The unavoidable consequence would be that they would be discouraged and think "it's not possible". We must therefore proceed differently. The following example illustrates how:

The emphasis of the training session is known: *The attack should be carried out across the wings more.*

- During the training emphasise the teamwork of midfield players and wingers. In preparation we analyse this teamwork and prepare a number of exercises for it. Let us take as an example a game phase from a points game. We look at it in all its elements, i.e. section for section and see what was right in it and what was wrong.
- Before the beginning of training we explain the coming exercises on the blackboard. We also discuss the hows and whys of the exercises. In this way the players are actively involved in the training.
- Furthermore we emphasise that the exercise should be carried out as realistically as possible. The players must pay attention to timing, accuracy, speed of the sequence of movements and to the element of surprise (in this order).

When we have analysed a move in the game, we see how complex it is. It is then not surprising that such a game pattern cannot be learnt immediately. The exercises must be structured in such a way that the intended move can, so to speak, be put together, whereby the players only move on to the next exercise when they have mastered the previous one. In doing so you proceed methodically in the following way:

1. *Timing:* The players carry out the movement without the ball, first slowly, then faster and finally at speed. After this brief progression, on the field the players know the sequence of the exercise.

2. *Accuracy:* The players carry out the exercises with the ball. The speed is gradually increased. In this way the accuracy of the execution of the exercise is maintained.

3. *Speed:* The aspect of speed now increases in significance, whereby of course timing and accuracy must not be forgotten. The objective is to be able to carry out the movement automatically at the desired speed.

4. *Surprise element:* Until now the exercise was practised in a technically clean form. We now call on the players to include an element of surprise so that we get as close as possible to reality. It is a good idea for the coach to let the players come up with their own "solutions". What they discover themselves they will also execute more easily. There are many options: feints, fake attacks, playing in unusual positions (e.g. a winger who attacks from a drawn back position) etc.

It is important that the players keep their real intentions secret as long as possible. Once we have come this far with the exercise, it is time to allow the players to execute it completely freely. The coach only gives the instruction: play across the wings.

Such a methodical approach results in the players also executing a task well when they are dealing with a real opponent. In this connection we must mention the part of the opponent in practising. A realistic execution of the exercise requires this (in games too the forwards must deal with defenders). Here, however, the coach should proceed in a well thought out way, otherwise this does not achieve much. If the defenders are not given concrete instructions then an exercise almost always ends with "kicking" and the associated risks. For this reason the coach should keep to the following pattern:

1. The exercises are first carried out without defenders.
2. We then add passive defenders. One can also first put up a few corner flags which function as passive defenders.
3. The exercise is carried out with active defenders without there being any serious struggle for the ball by the defenders. To a certain extent the defenders help structure the exercise.
4. Finally the defenders actively fight for the ball. Make sure, however, that at the beginning the defenders do not try too hard: no forward likes to be put out of action. It is exactly this which can lead to injuries at training.
This example makes clear that this training objective cannot be covered in a single training day. Take sufficient time. It is better to spend five weeks on it and then achieve real successes than to have the exercise fail through proceeding too hastily with the consequence that the game variants can simply be forgotten. It is not quantity that counts, but quality.

7 Practical Situations

The time of first getting to know each other is over and as coach we now know what player core is available. Our first worry is the training programme and getting to know the players. With the aid of our player filing system we can immediately note the first data. We probably know a number of the players a little better already so that their sheets already contain more information. In the course of the preparatory weeks you will get to know them all even better. Our annual programme will be the foundation for further preparations. Part 1 of this programme covers the pre-season from mid-July to the end of August. In mid-July the time has come for the coach and the troop of players to get to know each other. Keep this getting to know each other brief and informal. Explain to the players how you want to approach the soccer season ahead with them and give them the opportunity to get to know their coach. By doing this you can easily instruct them in the organisation of your training (time, punctuality, seriousness etc). All of these preparatory things of course require much thought and work. For each of be thematic points emphasised we will give you an example of how it can be done. Every coach can modify these examples according to his own views. In the following chapters you will find:

- the pattern of an annual programme with a number of explanations,
- a rough sectional training plan for the first period with a number of practical comments,
- a suggestion for preparing the players for the season,
- an organisational model of the training which follows the suggestion for preparing the players.

8 The Annual Programme

Division into periods

An annual programme puts you in a position to systematically get the players into form in such a way that they can maintain their fitness as long as possible. For this purpose we divide the season into various periods:

Pre-season
- Preparatory period (July)
- Build-up period (August)

High-season
- Soccer-specific training (September, October)
- Points game training (November to May)

Post-season
(transitional period, rest period) (June, July)

Preparatory period
(1st part of the pre-season)

In this period we create the foundations for the rest of the season. At the beginning we do not overdo it, but rather build up slowly.
Principle: Longer distances at low speed, e.g. two runs of five minutes each.
Execution: In game form (e.g. forest and cross-country running).

Build-up period
(2nd part of the pre-season)

We gradually pay more and more attention to technique (running, jumping), develop fighting strength, strength and speed ability (interval method) with load.
Principle: Shorter distances, fast execution.
Training means: Cross-country running and running on the field.

Soccer-specific training
(1st part of the high season)

The competitive games begin. Training is harder and concentrated on soccer.
Principle: On the basis of the level of fitness achieved we now work actively and deliberately on soccer.
Training means: Running training with the ball, technique training with the ball and once a week suitable fitness training with the emphasis on speed ability and strength.

Points game training
(2nd part of the high season)

A large part of points game training is aimed at maintaining a certain level of performance, developing strength and reducing weaknesses, all of this adapted to the circumstances.
Principle: Interval training with and without the ball, circuit training and special training.
Training means: Various running and ball exercises, group training.

Post-season
(transitional period, rest period)

The time to mentally recover and "fill up". Here a healthy way of life and active regeneration are important.

Planning

When working out an annual programme it is important to know which emphases determine training at what time. Table 1 and the chart that follows give an overview.

July/August Pre-season		September to May High season		June Transitional period
Preparatory period	Build-up period	Special perfecting of fitness with soccer-specific means	Competitive period	
General foundations, especially endurance	Period of soccer-specific training	Technique and training of tactics	Optimal use of ability trained (points game training)	Regeneration of mental and physical strengths

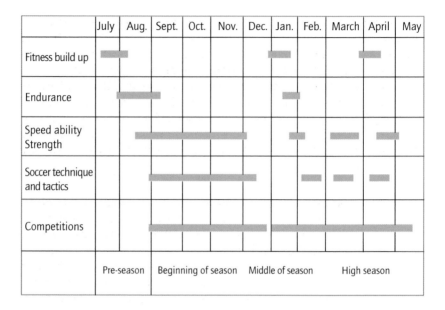

	July	Aug.	Sept.	Oct.	Nov.	Dec.	Jan.	Feb.	March	April	May
Fitness build up	▬					▬			▬		
Endurance		▬				▬					
Speed ability Strength			▬▬▬▬				▬	▬	▬		
Soccer technique and tactics			▬▬▬				▬	▬	▬		
Competitions			▬▬▬▬▬▬▬▬▬▬▬▬▬▬▬▬▬▬▬▬								
	Pre-season	Beginning of season		Middle of season			High season				

Suggestion for preparing players for the new season

Friends, although the points games have not yet begun, we already have one foot in the new soccer season. A season which will be long and hard. Therefore I have thoroughly prepared the preparatory phase so that we can start into the new season as well as possible. Because the time of the "technician" who didn't have to work very hard is practically over, we will adopt the principles of moving soccer: - playing without the ball, - the involvement of team mates, - support of team mates. In the same degree that training progresses we will develop a collective way of playing which will include everybody - both attacking and defending. We will develop automatisms so we know what we have to do and what our team-mates will do. Nevertheless the spontaneity of playing soccer will not be lost because each one of us can make use of our soccer abilities. In order to "playfully" learn teamwork, which is indispensable, we will play preparatory games. The game rhythm will of course be matched to physical fitness. We will not run onto the field to win, but rather to practise certain moves for the points game. In this way we will get to know each other best as soccer players. We won't burden ourselves with too much, but our way of playing will develop systematically to the degree that we get closer to the points games. Thus the first two preparatory games will be in the sense of games without the ball and clean passing on of the ball. This and no more. On this foundation we will achieve a tactically balanced game full of variety which involves everyone. Everyone must be punctual at training, at points games and any other meetings and turn up at the agreed time. No exceptions will be made. By the way, at the first training I will make an interesting suggestion. During the training as well I will constantly demand your full involvement.

Training will be diverse and serve the game. During the whole season we are dealing with a team game so don't let your team-mates down because of your lack of fitness. Don't look for excuses for being absent. In the season we'll go through thick and thin together. If there are problems or you have a question - before training I will always be available. You can always come to me. If you are injured, then report this before training if you think that you cannot train. It goes without saying that no one is to leave training without permission. Don't come to training in your tracksuit, but get changed in the changing room. And: never eat just before training.

I must also say something about my hobby horse: I know as a rule the points games are hard and many things happen which are not allowed. But on the playing field I do not want to hear any criticism of referees or opponents. Our motto must be: play and say nothing. We are no angels either and we will make it as difficult as possible for our opponents. If we play as we should it will be much harder for the opponents. More on this at training. We are heading towards the championships series with a certain objective. With me you will certainly not fall into hibernation. What we are attempting we can only achieve through hard work. If you sometimes think at training: "I can't keep this up", then think about your future opponents, they will be thinking the same thing. It is up to us to make this happen on the field now.

Any changes in the programme and the fixing of the later dates will be given to you at training. Training will always take place on Tuesday and Thursday evenings. For all squad players it is of course obligatory. Considering the training programme and the hard season ahead of us I ask you to let us know as soon as possible when you will take your vacations.

Organisation of training

In addition to the two weekly training sessions on Tuesday and Thursday, there are three more elements of the actual training, they take place 45 minutes before the game. These are the team talk, the warm-up phase and the last contact before the game.

General Training Overview
Beginning of training: Punctually at 7 pm
Training duration: About one-and-a-half hours
With regard to the demands on players, the training sessions are structured in such a way that they do not last longer than 90 minutes.
1. *Tuesday training* (generally fitness training)
a) 10 minutes of theory - talk in a relaxed atmosphere
- Discussion of the game on the previous weekend
- Positive aspects (to be maintained)
- Negative aspects (to be eliminated)
The things which are spoken about here are never directed at a particular person but are discussed only in a positive way to the benefit of the whole team.
b) Explanation of the training ahead
c) Warm-up
d) Main part of training
2. *Thursday training*
a) 10 minutes of theory: Discussion of the points game ahead
b) Explanation of the training ahead
c) Warm-up
d) Main part of training
3. *Sunday* (preparation for the game)
a) Tactical discussion 45 minutes before the game starts
b) Warm-up
c) Five minutes before the game begins, last contact on the playing field
Because this is a real training game and the players are supposed to be concentrating on the game, only a limited number of board members should be allowed into the changing rooms. It is expected of these gentlemen that they do not take part in the talks or intervene in any way. Only exception: announcements by the board. Note: Many clubs have their tactical talk on Fridays. In the meantime I'm trying to give you as much free time as possible. Before every training we will have a talk (theory) during which no one should be absent. We will therefore agree to turn up punctually on Tuesdays, Thursdays and also Sundays before the game each time so that we do not lose any time and can progress well in training. Before the warm-up (training and game) the ball will be left alone. I don't want to lose any players because of silly injuries. So, first warm up ... and then the ball.

Sample of a section plan for the first seven weeks

Date	Time	Programme	Material
A Getting to know the players			
B			
1. Tuesday 15. 07.	7pm	Exercises in the forest, getting to know each other in the break	Running shoes
Thursday 17. 07.	7pm	Running in the forest, theory	Running shoes
Sunday 20. 07.	10am	Cross-country running, theory	Running shoes
2 . Tuesday 22. 07.	7pm	Introduction to moving soccer	Soccer boots
Thursday 24. 07.	7pm	Training and game	(for the rest of
Sunday 27. 07.	10am	Training of both teams	the programme)
3. Tuesday 29. 07.	7pm	Fitness training	
Thursday 31. 07.	7pm	Soccer training	
Sunday 03. 08.	10am	Game A-team against X	
4. Tuesday 05. 08.	7pm	Fitness training (in game form)	
Thursday 07. 08.	7pm	Soccer training	
Sunday 10. 08.	10am	A-team against X (first tournament game)	
5. Tuesday 12. 08.	7pm	Soccer training	
Thursday 14. 08.	7pm	Soccer training	
Friday 15. 08	7pm	Training game	
Sunday 17. 08.	4pm	A-team against X (second tournament game)	
6. Tuesday 19. 08.	7pm	Fitness training	
Thursday 21. 08.	7pm	Game A-team against X	
Friday 22. 08	7pm	Special training for the defence players	
Sunday 24. 08.	4pm	X against A-team (third tournament game)	
7. Tuesday 26. 08.	7pm	Fitness training	
Thursday 28. 08.	7pm	Soccer training	
Friday 29. 08	7pm	Special training for midfield players	
Sunday 31. 08.	4pm	A - team against X (4th tournament game)	

Note: Exercise programme for the second team follows later.

9 Sport and Health

Warming up

In all sport it is important to prepare the body for the expected load. At the end of the day this leads to better training effects. We call this preparation warming up. Warming up means using the muscles and improving general blood circulation. Tests have shown that proper warming up considerably reduces the risk of injuries and muscle pains. With the warm-up beforehand we prepare the body for the coming loads. It is then better able to achieve performances. We divide warming up into active and passive warm-up.

a) Passive warm-up:

- Hot showers or hot and cold showers (e.g. 30 second hot and 10 second cold water)
- Relaxing massages of various muscle groups (using alcohol)
- Radiation using a heat source or infra-red lamp

b) Active warm-up

- Stretching and swinging exercises which use as many muscles as possible.

Each year a large number of sports participants suffer injuries of all kinds, including broken bones. Rapid help in the case of accidents and expert help with serious accidents should be left to those people trained in first aid.

Sport and nutrition

In every sport, energy requirements are of great significance. They are dependent on many factors, but also on the type and the intensity of loads and the specifics of the particular sport. Quantitatively and qualitatively appropriate nutrition as well as sufficient rest are very important. The most important elements of our diet are: Proteins, carbohydrates and fats.

1. Proteins: Proteins are made of amino acids and are the basic building blocks of the living cells. The body needs about 20 amino acids. When there is a lack of food the body can produce 12 itself (synthesise). The other eight are called essential amino acids. The biological value or valency of protein is determined by the content of essential amino acids. The valency of animal protein is generally greater than that of plant proteins. Example: Milk - 100%, meat - 80%, corn - 55%. If the proportion of proteins in food, above all of the essential and amino acids, is known, one can choose a favourable combination of foods.

Usually we need one gram of protein per kilogram of body weight per day. In the case of intensive sport, e.g. soccer, this requirement can increase by four times as much per day. If the protein requirement is covered, muscle strength, concentration and performance remain at an optimum. In addition, a protein rich diet also increases the basic metabolism of the body so that in the short term more energy can be made available.

2. Carbohydrates: Carbohydrates are usually consumed in the form of complex sugar (polysaccharides). Digestion ensures that this sugar is split into simple sugars (monosaccharides) such as glucose or fructose. This sugar is then stored in the muscles and liver in the form of glycogen. Because the glycogen stores in our body are limited, during the game monosaccharides in particular must be consumed. Complex sugars must be oxidised with the aid of oxygen. In sport this leads to a drop in performance. It is therefore most important to drink glucose rich drinks (fitness drinks) and eat carbohydrate rich food (calories) during or after intense sporting activity to ensure a rapid rebuilding of muscle glycogen.

3. Fats: Fats serve the storage of energy supplies: provision of energy for cell metabolism, solvents for fat-soluble vitamins (e.g. A, D, E and K). The short and long chain fatty acids are important. The polyunsaturated fatty acids (long) are of especial importance because the body cannot produce these itself, but must consume them with food. It is therefore of the greatest importance that after great loads a sufficient supply of calories is ensured. For this reason the proportion of fat in food may be increased.

4. Fluid Intake: A with good fluid balance is essential for our body. After all our body consists of 65% water, 2/3 of which is stored in the cells and 1/3 in the blood. Both too much and too little fluid lead to serious harm. Sporting activity is coupled with transpiration (fluid loss). This is a protective mechanism of the body, with which it can maintain a constant body temperature. If there is too much fluid loss our body gives us a signal (thirst) which shows that there is a fluid deficit in our tissue. It is an understandable but a false reaction to then drink quickly, in great quantities and cold. During sport this must always be avoided. In order to achieve a normal situation after load, the most important food elements must be consumed quickly. The fluids one drinks must be isotonic, i.e. they must contain the same amount of salt as blood plasma which leads to rapid passing through the stomach and absorption in the intestines (isotonic thirst quenchers).

5. *Minerals:* These are very important for the muscular and nervous system. Muscle cramps, dizziness and performance drops can point to a deficit in this regard. Many minerals are lost in particular through transpirational fluid. Essential minerals are calcium, chloride, potassium, magnesium, phosphor, iron and sodium.

6. *Vitamins:* Vitamins are organic compounds with a generally complex structure whose presence is necessary for proper functioning of the body. In general they do not develop in the body itself but must be consumed in food. Among others the vitamins A, B1, B2, C and D are important. Especially in the case of dizzy spells their effects can be felt quickly (nutrient tablets, muesli bars).

Length of time some foods remain in the stomach after eating:

- 1 to 2 hours: water, tea, cocoa, coffee, milk, clear soup, soft-boiled eggs
- 2 to 3 hours: coffee and cocoa with cream, hard-boiled eggs, boiled fish, white bread
- 3 to 4 hours: boiled rice, boiled beef, dark bread, apples
- 4 to 5 hours: roast meat, hot beans and peas.

This brief information has been provided because it is important to know what is going on in the body in view of the hard training and the games which the players must go through. These tips are meant as help in developing and maintaining fitness.

10 Beginning of Training

It is finally time: We are beginning with the first training of the pre-season. In the annual programme we have planned two periods for the pre-season:
- the preparatory period,
- the build-up period.
The aim is to improve the level of fitness. This occurs through
- the carrying out of long-distance runs at a slow pace
- general developing exercises.

For this purpose we seek an appropriate area, preferably with forest, sand tracks and a number of sandy areas. This kind of terrain can be found almost anywhere. This is where the first training should take place before we begin on the sports field. If such an area is not available, this first training can of course take place on the playing field, but experience shows that it is more monotonous on a playing field than in the forest. Once basic fitness has been built up again we can - still in the pre-season - begin with the more specialised fitness period (somewhat more oriented to soccer).

In doing so we gradually switch to technique (running, jumping etc) and load - speed ability (e.g. through interval training). The principle remains the same, but now we choose shorter distances at higher speed. The training means will mainly be forest runs or runs on the playing field. We can imagine these two periods schematically as pyramids. We begin below (short formula: "long duration and slow execution" and move upwards "short and fast"). Questions which must be asked during the preparation of every training:

Before training:
- What is to be taught?
- Why is it to be taught?
- How is it to be taught?

After training:
- Did the training fulfil expectations?
- Did the training have the desired result?

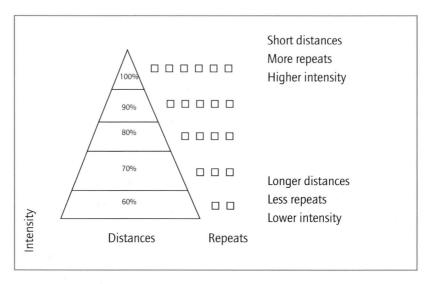

Short distances
More repeats
Higher intensity

100%

90%

80%

70%

Longer distances
Less repeats
Lower intensity

60%

Intensity

Distances   Repeats

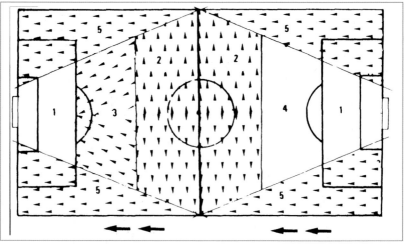

Theoretical evaluation of the individual playing-field zones

1 – Zone of truth

2 – Preparation and organisation zone

3 – Clearance zone

4 – Defence zone

5 – Free space

Note:

In practice the zones shift, depending on whether the team is on the attack or in defence.

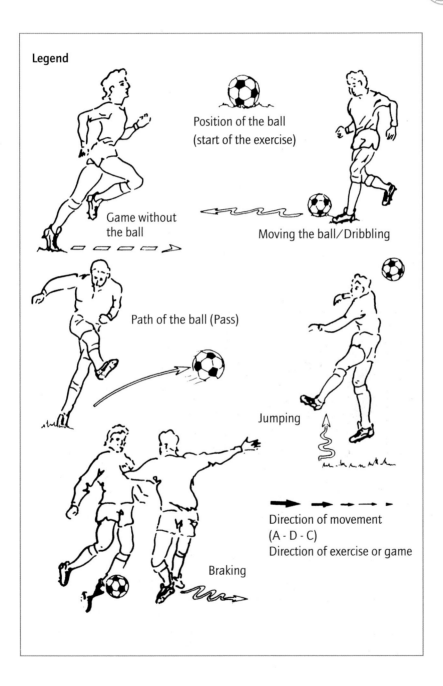

Legend

Position of the ball
(start of the exercise)

Game without
the ball

Moving the ball / Dribbling

Path of the ball (Pass)

Jumping

Braking

Direction of movement
(A - D - C)
Direction of exercise or game

11 Preparatory Period (Pre-season)

Training Session 1: The Forest as Sports Field

Basic principles

This first training is real fitness training. Do not demand too much of the players. We will stick to longer distances at low speed and a few running ABC exercises. We run at half power over distances of 100 m, 200 m and 300 m in alternation with sufficient recovery (walking, hopping etc). As a basis we will take three runs in five minutes.

Terrain

Preferably open field or forest. We particularly make sure we have ground with good traction. The terrain can also have areas with loose sand. The players should not, however, continually work on loose sand or hills.

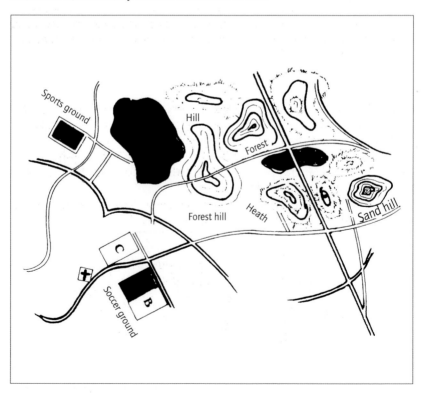

Organisation and procedure of training

- Everyone wears running shoes.
- We do not need any equipment for training.
- The preparatory warm-up takes place on the soccer field.
- On the way to the forest hills runs slowly (sand path).
- Descend to and run across an area of moor land to the sand hill.
- Exercises on the sand hill, run down the sand hill.
- Then we run to the actual forest hills (more hilly).
- On the flatter part of the forest hills we carry out a number of movement games.
- After that we train in the forest on very hilly terrain with ground with good traction.
- Come out of the forest easily.
- Cool-down run along the forest path and back to the starting point.

We have noted this data while exploring the area beforehand. Using the information on the location we work out the content of the training session. In doing so we always remember that this first training will be the first meeting of the players. The coach makes clear that the time of relative calm is over and that the time for training is beginning again.

Warm-up

Warming up is very important, especially in the early period of the pre-season. It takes place on Terrain A and lasts about 20 minutes, keeping to a very low pace. In warming up, as many muscle groups as possible are addressed, but the joints only marginally. These exercises are alternated with unwinding/loosening exercises.

Formation: Practice in rows of two across the whole width of the terrain, turn at the sideline and go back along the outside line.

To mark the load and recovery phases we work across the width of the field and return easily to the starting point. Then a new exercise follows.

Suggestion for a warm-up	
- Easy trot	- walk back
- Hopping run	- go back easily
- Run sideways (left, right)	- walk back
- Arm swings, circling backwards and forwards	- go back easily
- Run backwards	- walk back
- Hopping run	- go back easily
- Standing jumps (10 m), loosen up and again 10 m standing jumps	- walk back
- While walking over 5 steps forward bends, hands go to the ground, the next 5 steps upright, arms held high (continuously)	- hopping run back
- Loosen joints and legs (turns inwards and outwards)	- go back easily
- Skipping	- walk back
- Run off easily and increase the pace to a run at half strength	- walk back
- Tempo run across half the width at half strength	- go back easily
- Start at half strength and slow down	- walk back
- Run easily	- run easily
- Sprint across half the width	- go back easily
- A last sprint	- now go back really relaxed

During the loosening phases always breathe out well and shake out the muscles.

Main part of training

FIRST PART

After the preparatory warm-up we head out in the direction of the forest hills. As far as possible we keep the players together in rows of two. Using the data researched we have worked out the complete rounds in a lively and diverse way. To give you an idea of what is planned, you will find here a sketch of the running circuit with the necessary explanations.

Forest hill

- We run 200 metres on the sand path, then loosen up after that over 100 metres and carry on at a running pace (to position 2), from where we go in the direction of the forest. This is followed by running towards the forest. After 200 metres walk easily again, stay together.

- Now comes a kind of cross country run (3). We then continue further in the direction of the forest. There we run off to the right into the forest (4). After we have put the forest behind us, we walk to the right (5).
- Now a small forest hill (sandy ground) comes into sight. We turn off in this direction (6), run to the foot of the hill, walk up it and run down it with small steps (7). Briefly loosen up and run around the hill once.
- Carry on downhill until you reach the path and from here run to the next hill (8). Alternately run up and down the hill several times, walking in between (9).
- After a brief recovery phase we run along the trail through the moor land towards the playing field (10). After about 200 metres we reach a forest clearing, half of which we walk around, half of which we run. Following this we run through the forest (11) towards the playing field (school). When we get here, we recover briefly (12). Then without a break we run to the old soccer field (13).
- To provide variety we have planned a running game on this field (Hunter and Game). Here everyone can go wild (according to their level of fitness). After this game we cool down on the grassy area to the left of the field.

Hunter and game

The players are divided into two equally large groups. The first group (Hunters) try to catch the second group (Game). The catching is done by tagging someone. That person then stands still, he is out of the game. He can, however, be relieved by being tagged by a team-mate. The Hunters must always be moving and may not guard "their" Game. After about five minutes the game is stopped, those out of the game are counted and the groups change.

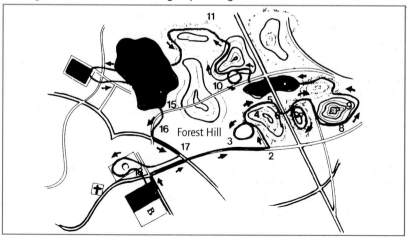

SECOND PART

- After this pleasant unwinding we move through the forest, alternately running and walking, in the direction of the playing fields (14). There we take the path behind the buildings (15). On reaching the field we briefly loosen up and then divide into two groups for a second playful "interlude".
- Hunter and Game (continuation)
- After finishing the game unwind and run through the forest to the entrance of the stadium.

  We cross the track (17) and then move in the direction of the soccer fields where we run a lap. Briefly relax and then divide into two groups against for a last "playful interlude" (18).
- Hunter and Game (continuation)
- After the game the players briefly remain loosely in motion (pulse under 100) and then go to the changing rooms.

It is obvious that you cannot and need not organise this training in exactly the same way. Using a practical example we have tried to show how you select a terrain and then make use of all its possibilities. Choose your own suitable terrain in plenty of time, one which is easy to reach, and try to organise the training sequence according to the paths and hindrances.

Training Session 2: Running in the Forest

Basic principles

This training calls for greater load through runs over shorter distances (50-75 m) at a higher pace as well as general developing exercises. The exercises are not yet carried out to the full. Include regular recovery phases. We carry on with 4 loads of 5 minutes each which are interrupted by gymnastic exercises. To achieve an optimum effect it is recommended to carry out this exercise at a slower pace.

Terrain

When we first got to know the circuit course, after a while we reached (position 12 in the previous sketch) a forest where the ground had good traction.

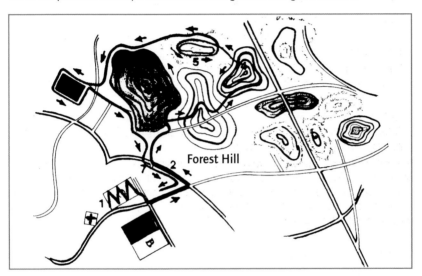

Organisation and sequence of training

- Everyone wears running shoes.
- No further materials are required for the training.
- Preparatory warm-up exercises take place on terrain C.
- Slowly run to the forest edge.
- In the forest various fitness gymnastics.
- Running exercises on the terrain.
- Run easily back to terrain C.
- Loosening exercises on terrain C.

Warm-up (1)

We repeat the warm-up we used in the first training. In order to get familiar with the various organisational forms, today we carry out the warm-up exercises in a line in sections (two lines across the width). This formation has the advantage that each player is subject to the same load and cannot "slack" as in a row. The lines in turn practise from sideline to sideline. When they reach the sideline each line stays in position, only the players turn 180 degrees so that now the second row is in front.

Main part

FIRST PART (2)

After the warm-up we start from the soccer field. As far as possible, the players run next to each other in pairs and staying in the group (good tractive ground for the feet).

SECOND PART (3)

On reaching the forest briefly loosen up and carry out a number of gymnastic exercises: slowly, from the feet followed by equally slowly springing back. Here are some examples:

Exercise 1: Side straddle stand, arms held up high. With outstretched arms bend the torso sideways, spring back twice. Carry out exercise several times in both directions.

Exercise 2: Crouch, hands on hips. Stretch the left leg to the side and spring back. Then right. Repeat several times.

Exercise 3: Go from standing to a crouch. Hands touch the ground. Spring back twice. Stand up, raise the arms up high and spring back twice. Repeat several times.

Exercise 4: Spread the legs slightly. Arms to the side. Right hand goes to the left foot and slowly springs back. Back to the starting position and then left hand to right foot and spring back. Repeat several times.

Exercise 5: Standing with arms held up high, forward bends with stretched legs, spring back. Repeat several times.

Exercise 6: Side straddle stand, arms at the side, turn the torso with outstretched arms, spring back.

After these stretching exercises we begin with two series of 4 running loads each in which each player practises on their own. At our command (call, or whistle) each player increases his pace (to 70%) and chooses his own direction. On the second command, relax. This load lasts about 8 seconds and the whole is repeated 4 times altogether. After a recovery phase (one minute) the second series follows. Between the various training sections we also include a few "interludes". An example: The players form pairs. Player A tries to shake off player B with feints. Player B on the other hand tries to follow as closely and quickly as possible. After 45 seconds the players exchange roles. Encourage the players during the game. We repeat this game until each player has had a turn twice. After this follows another brief relaxation phase.

THIRD PART (4)

We now shift our sphere of activity to position 4 and here practise in groups of four or five. The individual groups run around easily. At the whistle they increase their pace to 70% - keeping close together. This tempo run is complemented by a change of direction. At a second whistle stop the tempo interlude. We repeat this dash 4 times altogether. After a brief recovery of two minutes there is a second series. This is followed by several loosening exercises and a resting break, then we go with the group to position 5 where we again have another "playful interlude".

FOURTH PART (5)

At the hills we again train in a group. A series of sprints follows, to the hill and around the hill. Use the terrain in such a way that people also carry on running on the flat parts, down hill and between the trees. After the second series we carry out a number of stretching exercises with springing back. Before we carry on to position 6, there is another "playful interlude".

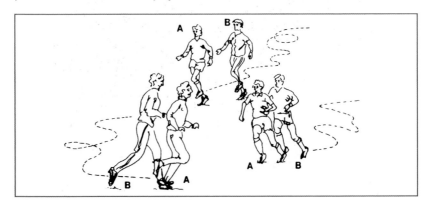

FIFTH PART (6)

When we have reached the flat area we get the players to practise in three groups. The players dash 50 m and then walk easily 25 m - 4 repeats in each case. After a resting phase start with a second series so that we have earned a two minute break. After this break the interlude follows again.

SIXTH PART (7)

We return to the sports field running easily through the forest where we repeat our "playful interlude" for one last time. We completely relax and loosen up (do not stand still). As soon as we have calmed down we go into the changing-rooms.

Training Session 3: Cross-country Running

Basic principles

The first two training days have passed easily and the lads have developed interest. Gradually we can increase the pace, but we must shorten the distances. In order to playfully improve general fitness, today we have additionally planned a number of active little games. Several hard sprints over short distances (25 to 50 m), with sufficient recovery in between, especially loosening exercises. At the same time make sure that the players do not stand still during the recovery phase.

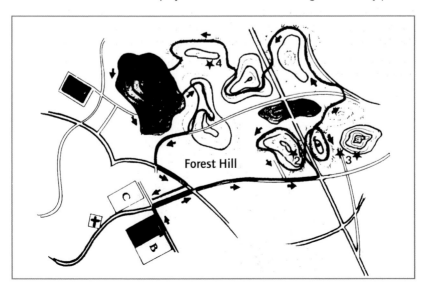

Forest Hill

Terrain

For today's training we will go into the now familiar forest once more, to be exact, to the sand hill. Here we sketch the options which we have chosen.

Organisation and sequence of training

- Everyone wears running shoes.
- For training we need one ball for every five players.
- The preparatory warm-up takes place on the soccer field.
- Warm-up run until the first bush on the left behind the hill (2).
- Training on natural running tracks.
- Training at the sand hill.
- Training in forest clearings.
- Finally a very intensive for at the sand hill.
- Come back out of the forest moving loosely.

Theory

Before starting, at the warm-up we get together with the players to make them familiar with a number of *principles of moving soccer.*

- We do not go on to the playing field in order to show a few tricks. Adequate technique is of course necessary, but only a means to the end.
- We do go on to the playing field to give our best from the first minute onwards.
- We attack the opponent according to our agreed plans.
- We move a lot without the ball with the intention of supporting and freeing up team-mates.
- Supporting our team-mates means: running a lot without the ball so that the opponent must react. By running free ourselves we give the person with the ball the opportunity to play the ball away.
- Free playing of a team-mate: anyone who runs a lot creates more options for the person with the ball. You can call for a pass and the person with the ball can also act more quickly and bring another team-mate into the game. After we have made the pass we do not stand still but get involved again.
- Proper passing on of the ball is made easier when the team-mates are running around freely. We have to chance a pass in time. If we are moving, the opponent has less time to get organised.
- Risk a goal shot.

We will adopt these basic rules in the games that follow.

Warm-up

Today we choose a new way of organising the warming-up exercises, which does not mean, however, that for every training we have to use a different organisational form. In the course of time every coach chooses certain organisational forms and uses them when they have proved themselves. We will test a number of basic forms so that we get to know their advantages and disadvantages. Today the formation is a large square with sides of 30 to 40 m. The players are divided into four groups and each group takes up position on one side of the square. Group A practises at the same time as Group B and Group C with Group D. The two groups standing opposite each other start at the same time and run towards each other. As soon as the groups have passed each other they slow down over the rest of the distance. When they reach the other side the coach gives the starting signal for Group C and Group D. Meanwhile Group A and Group B recover and then start again as soon as groups C and D have arrived (continuously). The advantage of this procedure is that everything remains very easy to see and takes place in an orderly fashion.

The exercises carried out during the rest of the warm-up are roughly the same as those of the previous warm-up. We finish this warm-up, however, with a series of running exercises with constantly increasing load and finish with 3 x 20 m sprints.

Main part

FIRST PART

After the warm-up we run at a fast pace from the sports field towards the sand hill (cross-country), where after a brief recovery we practise fast accelerations from a technical point of view. A "fast acceleration" is very important for soccer players who must frequently run short distances. It is often said of a player that he is fast or slow, but with a few technical improvements when starting, speed ability can certainly be improved.

When accelerating note the following:

- Begin with short strides.

- Systematically lengthen your strides until maximum speed is reached.

After the acceleration slow down, recover and repeat the whole thing several times. In the cross-country to be carried out later on we get the players to go full speed a few times and correct them if necessary.

SECOND PART

We divide the players into two groups of five to seven, each group gets a ball. Each group has one passer. We can make the exercise forms very active by getting the groups to carry them out in competition and awarding points. Then, however, we must make sure that all groups stand on a line. Here are some examples which you can of course adapt to your own ideas accordingly:

Exercise 1: P throws the ball to player A who then passes the ball on to the next person etc. The last player runs with the ball to the front (group quickly moves up), throws the ball to P who then throws it again. This is repeated until everyone has had a turn twice.

Exercise 3: Like Exercise 1, but the ball is passed over the players' heads.

Exercise 2: P throws the ball to A, who then sprints with the ball to the rear (group moves up). The ball is passed to the front and played back to P, who then throws the ball to the first man again etc. Each player has two turns.

Exercise 4: Like Exercise 1, but the ball is passed on by turning the upper body (feet stay in the same place).

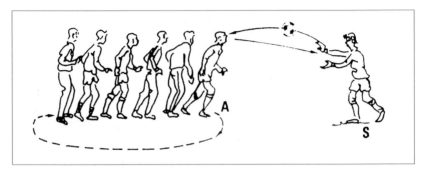

Exercise 5: P throws the ball to A who then heads it back and goes to the back (group moves up).

THIRD PART

To improve the ball and movement feeling of the players a handball game with two teams of six to eight men each is planned.

Game rules: Do not run with the ball in your hand, pass the ball on quickly, avoid touching the opponent and always keep moving without the ball as well.

Time: 2 x 7 1/2 minutes After a somewhat longer recovery phase we carry on - with the same team - with a kind of rugby game.

Game rules: As with handball, but now with body contact (although no kicking is allowed). At the whistle immediately stop everything.

FOURTH PART

After a pleasant unwinding we then cover the rest of the distance with short and faster sprints (and recovery phases after them). We finish training on terrain C with a number of loosening exercises. After we have calmed down a bit we go to the changing-rooms and then take a well earned shower.

12 Build-up Period (Pre-season)

Training Session 4: Moving Soccer

At the last training we spoke briefly about a number of important basic moves on which our game will be based in this season. Before warming up we will again discuss a number of important points about what makes up modern moving soccer. Moving soccer is: - playing without the ball, - rapid passing on of the ball, - involvement of team mates, - after the pass supporting team-mates.

You often see that when a player gets the ball all his team-mates dash off and call for the ball. The result is that the person with the ball often has difficulty getting the right pass while the "dashers" literally run into the arms of the defenders who only have to wait for them. The result: loss of the ball just at the moment when the team have left their positions. How can we do this differently?

• The players run in different directions and make sure that they can always be played to.
• The opponent is enticed out which creates free space for a team-mate.
• Certain players go towards the person with the ball. After the pass immediately run free and offer yourself.
• After the pass has been carried out, support players yourself.
We will not learn all of this in one day. Our collective game will develop, whereby certain patterns of behaviour will become automatic. You need to get to know each other and learn to play for each other.
Today as the first basic move of moving soccer we will deal with the principle: see - decide - play. After a long warm-up in which everyone participates well, for the rest of the training we will work with the ball. If everyone continues to give their best in training as they have so far, we will manage it.

Warm-up

Today we will do the warm-up in a rectangle of 30 m x 10 m (4 flagpoles at the corners). The players form up in 4 lines. In each group of four a leader is determined in the following way: in the first group it is the player on the outer left, in the second the player on the outer right etc. The prescribed exercises are carried out along the entire length of the rectangle. When they get to the other end the entire group turn off to the side of the leader (the players follow the leader), return to the sideline and join up at the back again. To ensure everything runs smoothly, the second group starts as soon as the first group is halfway to the turning point. This type of training requires of the coach a number of preparations and familiarity with the planned exercises, especially as these follow each other very quickly. Every time it is the turn of the group that started first, the coach describes the next exercise. This has the advantage that the exercises can take place very quickly and in an orderly fashion. The coach can keep everything well under control and maintains an overview. The players don't disturb each other and there is a good atmosphere because they see everyone around them doing the exercises. In this way a whole training session - with or without the ball - can be held. In order to use the rectangle as much as possible we will also carry out the second part of the training here, namely the fitness exercises. The exercises are as follows: Running, carrying, one-on-one, jumping and dashing.

WARM-UP PROGRAMME
Here is a complete warm-up programme without the ball. The exercises are numbered in order to give the sequence in which they are to be carried out:
1. Run easily (test runs for the leader), return and form up at the rear
2. Hopping run, come back easily
3. Run easily
4. Hopping run
5. Run easily raising knees
6. Hop, alternately in straddle and final position
7. Run easily
8. Walk, circle the arms forwards and backwards
9. Run easily with feet crossing in front of each other
10. Run backwards
11. Run easily
12. Run sideways
13. Run easily
14. Run sideways to the right

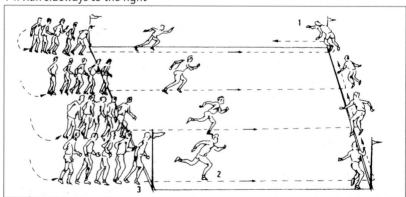

15. Shake legs
16. Hop on one leg (alternately left and right, 5 steps each time)
17. Run easily
18. 5 steps forward bends, hands on the ground, 5 steps with straightened torso, arms above and spring back
19. Run easily
20. Run and jump (5 times at the command of the leader)
21. Run easily
22. Run with a jump and header (5 times at the command of the leader)
23. Run easily
24. Run and sprint 10 m (at the command of the leader)
25. Start running, increase pace and slow down
26 Dash, slow down, recover, regulate breathing.

The players keep moving (walking) and remain disciplined because directly after the recovery phase there is a fitness training session on the same field.

Main part

FIRST PART: FITNESS TRAINING

After our intensive warm-up, we get our rhythm again in order to begin with our fitness training.

1. Run up 15 m, at a sign from the leader the group dash to the end of the rectangle, come back easily and get their breath back.
2. Acceleration from a standstill, slow down.
3. Run backwards 20 m, at the command of the leader turn and sprint to the end.
4. Sprint the entire distance (to the last metre).
5. Run easily.
6. Acceleration from a standstill to the line - who will be first? Now follows the section "carrying", here the players practise in pairs.
7. Player A carries player B (in front of his chest) over the entire distance, come back easily, shake out arms.
8. Now player B carries player A.
9. Piggyback, walk back easily.
10. The same exercise, but with role swap.
11. "Wheelbarrow" across the entire field.
12. The same exercise, but with roles swapped. Now follows the section "one-on-one", the players are still practising in pairs.
13. Players A and B run next to each other, barging by A which is absorbed by B.

14. The same exercise, changeover.

15 The same exercise, but now player A barges alternately from left and right.

16. The same exercise for player B.

17. Players A and B are about 1 m apart, player A falls into the arms of B, player B pushes A back and A brakes a little.

18 Change.

19. Players A and B run sideways chest to chest, at the command of one of the two players jump with chest contact.

Now follows the section "Jumping", the players still practise in pairs.

20. Leapfrog.

21 Run easily, five times powerfully jump up high.

22. The same exercise but now with a header.

23. Sprint over the entire length - who will be first? (2 to 3 times)

24. Dash over 10 m, reduce pace (10 m), increase again (twice and recover).

SECOND PART: IN FOURS WITH THE BALL

Our goal is to learn the basics rules of moving soccer: see - decide - play. Before we get the ball, but on getting the ball at the latest, we must already know how we will continue the game. The exercises which will now follow will be repeated 3 times. The first time slowly, but very accurately (getting to know them). The second time faster, but we still pay attention to correct execution. The last time as fast as possible but this time pay attention to the correct pass into the free area. The players are numbered from 1 to 4.

Exercise 1: Player 1 has the ball. At a command he stops the ball and dashes away. Player 2 dashes towards the ball at the same command and takes it over. The other players move around unattached. This is carried on until each player has had the ball 4 or 5 times.

Exercise 2: Like Exercise 1, but now 1 cleanly plays the ball to 2 (low or medium high); this player must also offer himself.

Exercise 3:

Exercise 4:

Exercise 5:

Exercise 3: Like Exercise 2, but now player 2 runs on in such a way that he can be played to in the open area. Make sure you offer yourself in time (acceleration).

Exercise 4: Now freely pass the ball as a group of four without paying attention to the order. To start with first call out the name of the player to whom the ball will be passed. All players move about and ensure clean passes.

Exercise 5: Like 4, but now with passive opponents (first 2, then 4).

Training Session 5: Game Without the Ball (Preparation)

Theory

No one in the team is tied to a fixed position. Nevertheless all positions must be occupied. Therefore: If a team-mate goes forward (everyone should have the courage to do so), his place should always be taken or secured. Which elements can we use in moving soccer? Obviously not everybody dashes around during the whole game just for the sake of "moving". The running around must have a purpose. It should - create surprise elements: sudden appearance of a player and making room for team-mates; - structure the game variably: shift the game and alternation of short and long passes. In order to do this we must play without the ball. In order to involve a team-mate in the game it is necessary that he makes himself available by suddenly running free (play without the ball) or that he gets the person with the ball to play to him in the free area (which has been created for him by a team-mate). It is also important that the player without the ball creates a game situation (by calling for the ball, going in deep, drawing the opponent with him to create space etc.). Therefore we keep to certain basic rules such as e.g.:

- For *defence:* Organisation of the defence, interruption and stopping of the opposing attack, supporting the build up of one's own team's attack (first building up pass) and, if the opportunity arises, suddenly going completely into the attack.
- For the *midfield:* Build-up of the attack, support during the attack, interception of the opposition's attack, when in possession of the ball involve team-mates in the game and shoot at goal from the second row.
- For the *attack:* Carry out own attack, on losing the ball disrupt immediately in order to force the opponent to over-hastily (incorrectly) pass; always keep the defenders busy by changing positions.
- For *all:* Moving up with team-mates is right, but always remember: the further you move up, the further you have to run back, and you have to last the whole game. Avoid too much individual risk, for your own team forms up for the attack, and if the ball is lost suddenly the team is not spread out in the defence.
- *The pass:* When your team-mate's speed is low, the ball must be played on the foot, i.e. almost to the man (body height). The greater the pace, the further in front of the player the ball must be played.
- *Moving up:* Can take place in various ways: into a free zone, as a sudden take-off attempt and as a dash behind the opponent (change of pace).

Our playing system of course puts high demands on every individual player. In any case the role of a defender is not limited to merely deactivating his direct opponent. A defender on the wing or even the sweeper will move up immediately if the opportunity arises and suddenly turn up in the space which has been left open for him by the attacker. For the next training a preparatory game is planned. Then we will have the opportunity to use the game without the ball in practice. The task which we give the players will be restricted to running free and offering themselves

as well as passing correctly (playing the ball on). In today's training as well we will teach playing without the ball (change of direction, change of pace) and, if all moves quickly, we will put what we have learnt into practice in a short game. After warming up we first take a test of physical condition, which, by the way, we will repeat monthly, so that we know of each player exactly what level his fitness has reached .

Warm-up

We warm-up intensively because during training considerable physical load will be required. Organisation as in the first training session: in groups of two across the width of the field.

Cooper Test

Without getting too scientific, it can be said that the Cooper Test is a way of estimating the physical condition of a person: within 12 minutes as great a distance as possible is run. Each player determines his own pace. We not only note the running distance in each case, but also register the heart rate after the final command as well as after 1 minute and after 5 minutes (each player does this himself). Note all data. The running distance covered should be about 3000 to 3300 metres (9 to 11 stadium laps).

Resting phase

Five minutes of recovery, measure heart rate. Under no circumstances keep still, sit down or lie down.

Soccer exercise forms

We divide the players into groups of 5 or 6. Each group works on its own. Nevertheless make sure that the groups do not disturb each other.

Exercise 1: Each group moves along the length of the field at medium pace. Regularly intercept the path of team-mates. It is best to run on behind the man (repeat 3 to 4 times). Then execute it once at a high pace.

Exercise 2 ➡

Exercise 3

Exercise 2: Like Exercise 1, but with increased speed at the moment the direction changes. Alternately cross over. Also execute once at a high pace.

Exercise 3: Like Exercise 2 but now change more quickly. Changes of direction and pace follow each other quickly. As a last variant: all groups show how fast and how well they can execute this exercise. After these preparatory exercises without the ball we repeat exercises 1, 2 and 3 one after the other, but this time with the ball.

• In the exercises the initiative comes from the man with the ball. He calls the name of a team-mate. This person dashes free so that he can be played to and receives a pass into the free area. The rest of the group end the exercise with a sudden change of pace and the exercise can be repeated (continuously).

• Only when Exercise 1 is mastered well should the next exercise be commenced, because the pace is greater there.

• As soon as the group can combine quickly alternating changes of direction and pace, it is time to involve a number of opponents in the exercise, e.g. an exercise form of 4 versus 2. The opposing players behave passively. They do not attack directly, but brake and hinder the game of the others. Those in possession of the ball should eliminate the opponents by virtue of their numerical superiority. The emphasis is purely on freely playing through pace and direction changes as well as clean passes at the right moment. To finish we organise a game with two equally strong teams (e.g. 6 versus 6) on half a large field (with two small goals of 1 m), in which what we have learnt is put into practice. The task is: The team in possession of the ball attacks. The player who can run free is brought into the game. The team which has lost the ball only defends passively and tries to get the ball again by disrupting the opponent with skilful placement of the team members (provoking a bad pass).

Training Session 6: Preparatory Game

Theoretical preparation

The coming preparatory game must be seen as a continuation of the last training. We finished training session 5 with a number of attack variants against a passive defence. Today we are dealing with an active opponent to whom our intentions are of no interest at all. It is "only" a second class opponent. But nevertheless... Today's task is very simple: we put into practice what we have seen. This means:
- playing without the ball
- clean passes
- using every opportunity for a shot at goal.
When we master that, we can carry on.

Practical preparation

- Explain to each player what his position is.
- Do not forget the reserves.
- Begin to warm up easily.
- Go up to each player personally and briefly explain to him the objectives and his particular responsibilities.
- In the case of the goalkeeper it is best to work with him actively yourself.

As coach we now have the opportunity to use our analysis sheets.

Preparatory game

Rule-of-thumb: In the first half, emphasis on the playful elements, in the second half: struggle through, task: moving without the ball and actions where the ball is safe.

Post mortem

We did not fail the "exam": the will was there. The main objective was clear and we shouldn't ask too much at once. We have already tried to combine, but we should not make it too difficult for ourselves. It is important that we have the courage to shoot from the second row. Although we scored some goals there is still plenty to do. After all, it was an easy opponent. A real competition game is of course different.

- Development of automatisms: Support of the forwards and support of the midfield.
- Defenders on the wing: Go into position on the inner side of the opponent, in the case of offensive midfield players go with them, stop the attack and, once in ball possession, build up again.
- Do not go to the ball with two, three players. One player goes to the ball, the others move up when he is in possession and cover if the ball is lost. When we are in possession of the ball we must have the courage to get away from the opponent.
- Do not only play with short passes, but structure the game variably.

Analysis sheet
Of the game .... (preparatory game)

Important phases	Central points	Notes, explanations
What moves the game on (ball possession). What stops the opponent's attack (loss of the ball)	1. Good positional play 2. Good execution 3. Intervention 4. Individual game 5. Collective game	
Is the ball kept in our own ranks?	Yes but positional play leaves a lot to be desired. Ball is kept by one man too long. Too many one-on-ones when in ball possession.	Improve game without the ball. More free running, also go across the width of the field sometimes.
Are we playing offensively?	Yes but at the price of safety. Everyone wants to attack (loss of strength when coming back). Agreements!	Somebody has to stay back. Move up more often and surprisingly.
Do the midfield/defence move up when the team is in ball possession?	Right defender is involved in the attack O. K. Midfield player must then temporarily take on his tasks.	Do not go up too often (surprise element is lost then).
Does the "Attack" defend when the ball is lost?	Stops too quickly when a pass is bad. Better to watch out when a backward pass or defence ball comes.	Disrupt longer in order to put the opponent off. Move back more quickly when the ball is lost.
Are the three rows maintained?	1st half: Yes, good. 2nd half: Not so good. Distance from each other: defence moved up well.	Very important; was often very good. Pace was not too high.
Positional play - individual - collective	Yes (but not yet automatised). There was a risk that too many players went along.	Slow but good. Brake better when the ball is lost (time).
Is the moving up of the opposing defence made use of?	They come back in a line, therefore bring someone from the 2nd (3rd) row into the game.	Occasionally move the ball forward yourself in order to avoid an offside trap.

Do not leave the inner defenders so free.
Use the last man more quickly.

- Do not immediately play in depth; make sure there is diversion on the wings.
- When a player calls for the ball, the pass must not necessarily go to this player but only if he is in a favourable position. Example: Player X calls for the ball on the right side. The player with the ball would then have to go directly towards the defender and at the last minute make a good pass to the wing (defender can no longer go back) or act as if he is making a pass and then march on (defender loses position).
- Do not get stuck in the corners of the field.
- After goal shots you have to follow through.
- If you think you are offside: never stop, but keep playing until the whistle blows.

Training Session 7: Fitness Training

The preparatory programme which we have carried out so far had the objective of getting the players physically used to the loads. This preparatory period has the advantage that the more difficult training sections which now follow can be better and more actively taken on and processed. Furthermore we have avoided the mistake of subjecting them to load too early and too much which can later easily lead to injuries. If the players have sore muscles the day after training this does not mean that training was good. The dosage of load during training was then not right.

The club of course has lots of training and friendly games on the programme which should be won if possible. We won't bother too much with them and use these games as game-technical and tactical training. Today for the first time we have - as we call it - the first real fitness training, which can be quite strenuous.

Theory

Thanks to the preparatory games we played and the observations we were able to make, we now have sufficient material for a short discussion with the players. Draw the really concrete things from the post-mortems and go through them briefly and concisely, preferably using an example.

Warm-up

We carry out a "classical", longer warm-up in which we try out a new organisational form. The players practise in two lines, they move across the field as a snake. The players in the second row snake past the person in front at a short distance (10 m), this person then carries out the same movements (alternating). These movement forms give the warm-up a character which corresponds to the following fitness training.

Exercise 1:

The players run easily towards the coach, spread out wide. At a signal from the coach they dash in the direction shown (7 times 10 m). Options: Left, right, forwards, backwards, diagonally, stopping (arms up), hopping while crouching (arms pointing down) etc. Also vary the duration of the recovery times.

Exercise 2:

In pairs. A varies running pace and direction (as in Exercise 1), B shadows him. After 3 minutes change.

Exercise 3:
The same exercise but now player B has the initiative. He suddenly dashes past player A and tries to shake him off (change of direction, change of pace, etc). Player A keeps as close to player B as possible. After sufficient recovery change roles.

Exercise 4:
Like Exercise 3, but now player A runs backwards. He reacts as quickly as possible to actions of B. Break, then change.

Exercise 5:
Like Exercise 4, but now B tries to get past A using a body feint. Player A prevents that by reacting to feints from B. B tries to get A out of his rhythm with a fast succession of body feints. After 30 seconds, changeover (each player three times).

Recovery

After every three exercises, take a short break. Start with a minute, gradually extend.

Exercise 6: Combination of Exercises 4 and 5: After a body feint, player A runs past B and dashes off, B turns around and pursues A.

Exercise 7: Jump up in pairs, chest contact in the air. One of the two players gives the command for the jump.

Exercise 8: With the ball. The two players move at a distance of 10 m apart and play the ball to each other, first moving forwards and backwards (accordion), then move to the side. Execute each pass cleanly.

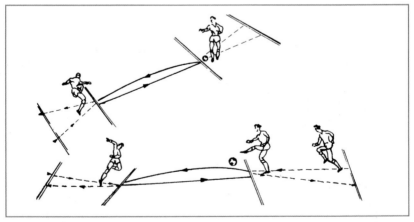

Exercise 9: In pairs. Passes according to the accordion principle: alternately long and very short - at speed.

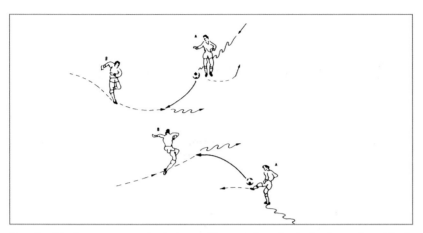

Exercise 10: Pass to a running player. Player A has the ball, player B suddenly accelerates and calls for the ball. Player A - paying attention to B's pace - accurately plays the pass to B, then A dashes on (alternating).

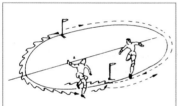

Exercise 11: In a circle. Player A plays the ball along the circle line, B runs in the opposite direction and takes over the ball from A. Both players maintain their direction.

Exercise 12: The same exercise, but now both players turn around after the ball has been taken over.

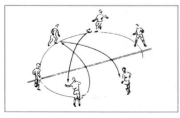

Exercise 13: Groups of six to eight. The players stand in a circle and pass the ball to each other (first call the name of the player for whom the ball is meant).

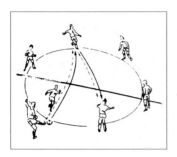

Exercise 14:
The same exercise. The player who gets the ball calls the name of another player, passes the ball, sprints after the ball and takes over his place.

Exercise 15:
In a group (form up in a circle) players try to keep the ball in the air as long as possible using headed passes in the air.

Training Session 8: Fitness Training in the Forest

In view of the great heat the training will be carried out in the forest. Here we can train in the shade and better avoid over straining.

Organisation and sequence of training

- Warm-up on the way into the forest hills.
- Group training in the forest. We need two flagpoles per group (4 or 5 players)
- Training in the area of the old field.
- Relay games.
- Group training on the hill.
- Training on sandy ground.
- Recovery phase.
A sketch of the area and the features used follow for better orientation.

Warm-up

On the way to the training area we have the opportunity to have a good warm-up. Work in a snake line or with 180 degree turns so that the last become the first and monitoring is easier.

1. GROUP TRAINING IN THE FOREST

On reaching position 1 the forest is in front of us. We run from the edge of the forest into the forest (c. 200 m), turn and return.

Exercise 1: Running (50 m) - recovery in alternation (not yet full speed). Four times there and back. Relaxing exercises after each series.

Exercise 2: Like Exercise 1 but now increase to sub-maximal speed over 30 m. Four times there and back.

Exercise 3: Like Exercise 1, but now in a zigzag over 20 m, increase pace. Four times there and back.

Exercise 4: The same exercise, but this time avoid the trees with short body feints. Include as many trees as possible.

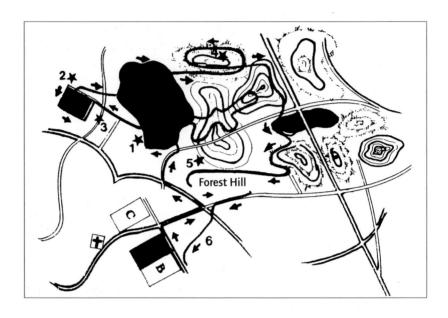

Forest Hill

Exercise 5:
Quickly run around the tree and then accelerate over 10 m.

Exercise 6:
Running - body feint, and from this movement start a sprint.

2. TRAINING IN GROUPS OF FOUR AROUND THE SOCCER FIELD
Five or more groups spread themselves out at equal distances around the edge of the soccer field. All groups start moving easily. At a command Group 1 start a relay: when they reach Group 2, this group starts, Group 1 takes a rest, etc. After the relay three minutes break while we prepare the next exercise.

3. REVERSE RELAY (3)
The groups remain unchanged. They form up in rows next to each other. Distance to turning point: 15 m. Each player runs eight times.

4. GROUP TRAINING ON THE HILL (4)
On the hill we determine a turning-point (tree). The groups move easily, at a command the first group sprints up, runs around the turning point and comes back (taking their time). Then the second group starts etc. (each group three times). Who will achieve the best time?

5. RUNNING GAME ON SANDY GROUND (5)
The game "Hunter and Game" (cf. first training session) seems appropriate. Each group has two turns at being hunter.

6. WINDING DOWN (6)
Walk easily through the forest back to area C and changing rooms.
Exercise 1: Reverse relay without additional movement tasks.
Exercise 2: Carry your partner piggyback - there and back (change at the turning point).
Exercise 3: Run backwards on the way there, forwards on the way back.

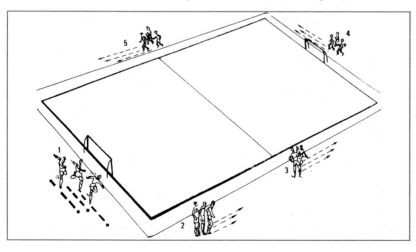

Training Session 9: Handball and Rugby

The players had already asked several times for a return match for the handball and rugby game (especially the latter) which they had played in the third training session. As such games are very good for improving fitness, we will grant this request today. The advantage of this kind of fitness training is that the players completely expend themselves and give their best without being conscious of it because after all these are games and they like playing them. The coach must, however, ensure order in the games (especially in rugby games).
We only need two balls - preferably small ones.

Warm-up
On the way to the hill we have plenty of time to carry out an extended warm-up.

Main part
On location we mark out a playing field in the sand and if necessary clear it of glass etc.

HANDBALL
Game duration: 2 x 20 minutes.
Game rules: Do not run with the ball in your hand, no physical contact.
Emphasis: Running free, playing away the ball after reception.

RUGBY
Game duration: 2 x 20 minutes.
Game rules: Game rules of handball do not apply, attacking with the feet is banned.

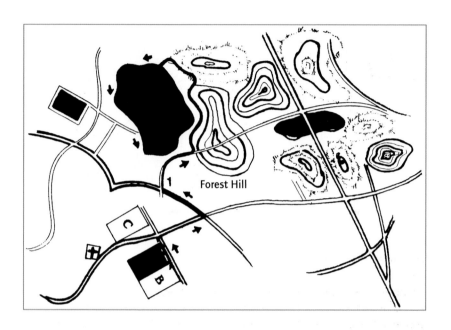

Training Session 10: Preparatory Game

In order to get a practical insight into the preparation of games and to encourage the use of the analysis sheets we will now cover a practical example in detail.

General tuning in

Today we have a preparatory away game against a fairly strong opponent. Today's task is: to build up the attack from a well organised defence and to a certain extent let the opponent come in the midfield in order to create space for counter-attacks. Today we will already fully utilise the principles of moving soccer.

Special tuning in

- Make clear to the defence that we don't just want to play defence, but rather to build up the attack from our own half.
- Midfield: When the ball is lost there is a buffer player who plays in front of our defence. When in possession of the ball, run around freely so that a player can quickly be played to.
- Explain to each player his role (not too many responsibilities).
- Warm up well and then remain active with the players.
- Have the courage to shoot at goal - use every chance.

Preparatory game

Basic rule: Approach it like a points game - preparation for the tournament game on Sunday.

Task: By playing without the ball and playing together create opportunities, without taking too great a risk.

Post mortem

General Assessment

The opponent - with a home advantage - played a kind of "kick and rush" soccer. On losing the ball they shot the ball away as far as possible. They fought for every ball and once in possession the ball was brought into the area close to the goal as quickly as possible with long through balls.

1st Half
* We allowed ourselves to be taken aback somewhat and reacted hectically so that we had to fight for the ball too much and there were too many ball losses.
* Once in ball possession, the ball was played across in the midfield too often without gaining ground.

Half-time: We must keep calm and in spite of the difficulties try to develop our own game. Don't just play away, but have the courage to build up the game. The midfield must be bridged more quickly. We expect more initiative from all players.

2nd Half
* We were able to put on a much better show.
* At times very good build-up (thus also opportunities created).
* When we get possession, kick simple passes (safe) and then suddenly force the game on.
* Shift the game more often - the opponents' defence then has to change coverage every time, through which gaps and thus also opportunities can arise (see goal).
* On Sunday in the tournament game we will manage it. But watch out, we are playing away against an opponent from lower class who will play the game of his life against us!

AIDS WHEN TRAINING

It should be mentioned that our club has a ball machine. This is a device which can be regulated automatically (many know such a device from tennis training), which because of its numerous functions can no longer be done without and has become a valuable aid for training. At first we were a bit sceptical of this robot, but thanks to its high degree of effectiveness and simple

use the ball machine was included in every training session within a very short time, both in technique/tactics and in fitness training. Because this device will become an accepted aid of coaches within a few years, we will briefly look at this. Every soccer coach knows that only regular repetition of the same movement sequences allows the players to learn the standard form of a game move or a system and make it their own. Here we are still not even taking the learning of basic techniques into consideration. Automatisms are developed only through many repetitions, whereby every player knows what will happen and where the ball will come to. Let's be honest, the effectiveness of the best exercise form or the best training schedule is destroyed by inaccuracies in the play-off. Bad passes disrupt rhythm and concentration.

Analysis sheet
of the game .... (preparatory game)

Important phases	Central points	1	2	3	4	5	Notes/explanations
What moves the game on (ball possession). What stops the opponent's attack (loss of the ball)	1. Good positional play 2. Good execution 3. Intervention 4. Individual game 5. Collective game						
Is the ball kept in our own ranks?		Yes	Slowly	o.K.	7 o.K. 4+/-	satisfactory	Too many balls "announced", too little variation
Are we playing offensively ?		Slowly	Yes	o.K.	o.K.	satisfactory	Attacks too slow
Do the midfield/defence move up when the team is in ball possession?		satisfactory	Yes		o.K.	Sometimes	Move up, but too often without a surprise effect
Does the "Attack" defend when the ball is lost?					Yes		Very good
Are the three rows maintained?				o.K.		o.K.	Panic too quickly - defence dissolves; this leads to problems in the midfield
Positional play - individual - collective gone		Sometimes		o.K.		Sometimes	Yes, but too "stereotype"
Is the moving up of the opposing defence made use of?							This opponent does not move up; hits everything away.

How many balls from ten attempts land where they should land (head, chest, foot, ground)? How many through passes upfield land where they are not expected? Above all when practising corner and free kicks these inaccuracies become obvious. Here the value of a ball machine becomes clear. Through the various possibilities we achieve a greater degree of effectiveness - without the players losing time by waiting for the right pass -, which leads to the coach being able to carry out his tasks more efficiently. It goes without saying that such a device cannot replace the coach.

Here briefly are some of the functions:
• The device can take up to 25 balls.
• It can be regulated with regard to
- strength of the shot (from soft to really hard)
- the height (from low to lob)
- the time between the shots (every 4 seconds)
- the length of the passes (5 m to 50 m)
- the side on the ball (left or right, with exactly determinable landing spot)
- the angle setting (various passes to various spots)
- most important: accuracy.
In the course of the season we will regularly slip in a few exercises which are carried out with the "jet ball", exercises which, however, can also be carried out just as well without the ball machine.

Training Session 11: Fitness Training between Corner Flag Poles

General

Today we have a very strenuous training ahead of us. You would do well to use your stopwatch to note the time. For the coach it is a very clear training which only requires few preparations on the field. The players practise in pairs on a predetermined field which is marked with two flagpoles (cones or similar). One player practises while the other "serves" and can take a break while doing so

Warm-up

We use the flagpoles which have been set up on the training area.
Organisation: We work across the width of the field and form the rows in such a way that one player stands in front of every row of flagpoles (e.g. rows of six).

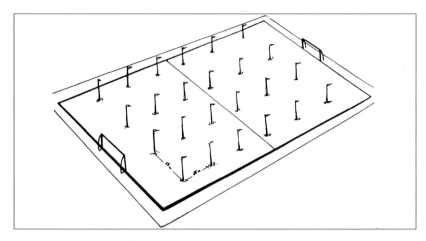

a) without the ball:
Slalom around the flagpoles; avoid the flagpoles - sprint from one pole to another; walk back and recover while doing so etc.

b) with the ball:
Alternately with the right and left foot, dribbling around the poles; avoid the poles (body feint); accelerating runs with the ball at the foot, kick the ball on a few metres and sprint after it etc. The warm-up exercises end with a series of various sprint exercises.

Main part

During the recovery phase the players divide up into groups of two and take a ball. In order to familiarise them with the exercise sequence you get each of them to run twice - starting between two flagpoles - one after the other round the flagpoles, each time going back to the starting point.

FIRST PART

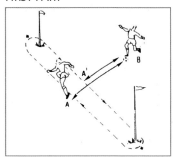   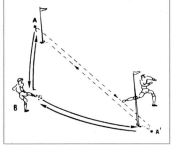

Exercise 1   *Exercise 2*

Exercise 1: Player B, in ball possession stands to the side of two poles, about 12, 13 m apart. At a command A sprints from one pole to the other, receives the ball and immediately plays it back, dashes on, turns around the pole, gets another etc.

Exercise 2: Like Exercise 1, but now player A receives the pass while running around the pole (on the outside), plays it back and sprints to the other pole, receives a pass etc.

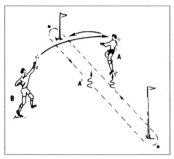

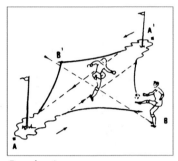

Exercise 3   *Exercise 4*

Exercise 3: The two previous exercises can be carried out in exactly the same way with one's head. Player B throws the ball. Make sure that the ball is not thrown too early.

Exercise 4: Wall pass (one-two) game. Player A starts at the pole with the ball at his foot, plays a wall pass (one-two) to B, receives the ball back, dribbles around the flagpoles and repeats the exercise to the other side.

SECOND PART: EXERCISES ACROSS THE WIDTH OF THE FIELD

As soon as the first pair have covered a third of the distance, the second pair starts etc.

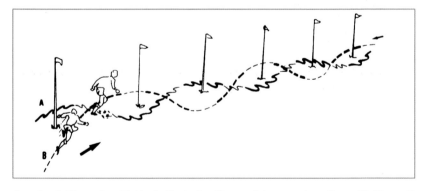

Exercise 1: Player A, with the ball, starts off on a slalom run together with Player B. On reaching the flag poles increase speed each time. Player B dashes, also changing pace, making sure that he keeps behind A. Come back easily and repeat three times.

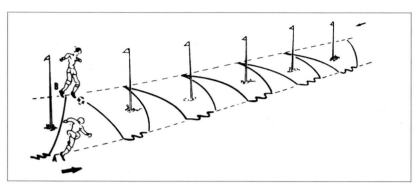

Exercise 2: Players A and B run at a distance of 7 m from each other. The ball is played backwards and forwards (at the beginning receive safely, later played back directly and increase the pace). Repeat three times.

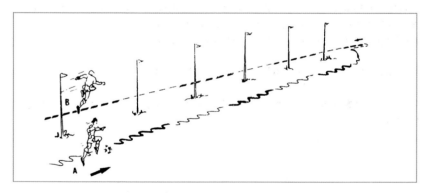

Exercise 3: Both players again start out parallel to each other, but now one player keeps the ball. Emphasise changes of pace.

THIRD PART
Relay competitions with several groups of six. The distance between the poles is 30 m.

1.) Running (and changing) is always done in pairs (three times altogether).
- Each runs individually (three times altogether).
- Pairs run, of which, however, after each round only one is relieved, until each player has run three times.

Considering that this exercise form is the close of training, it is best done as a competition for which points are given (1st place: 5 points, 2nd place: 4 points etc. per round). A recovery break follows. The players recover actively. Then gather up the materials (make sure the flagpoles are not used as spears).

Training Session 12:

Circuit Training with Soccer-specific Exercises

After the two positive preparatory games we can - using the data gathered - better plan the next steps. A major part of our weekly training we used for exercises which encourage later automatisms. For this, good training organisation, which ensures high exercise density, is a major prerequisite for a great training effect. A way of using the exercise time rationally is the following form of exercise organisation: We divide up the exercises to be carried out on the field in such a way that the exercise stations - beginning with Exercise 1 - form a kind of circle. Because we only have a small group of players (2 to 4 people) per station, who simply move to the next station when they have finished their exercise, during the entire training they are working calmly and continuously. For the sake of order, we must, however, make sure that at a signal (sign that the exercise is finished)

- the equipment (balls etc.) is taken back to its place,
- the groups move on to the next exercise station,
- and, arriving there, immediately start with the next exercise.

When there is good organisation and preparation, training takes place which is clear for the coach, and in which the players are continuously working and concentrate on their exercises.

Note: If we place the emphasis on accuracy, then it is a technical training which must not be too strenuous. If the emphasis is on speed ability and speed of execution, then training load is higher.

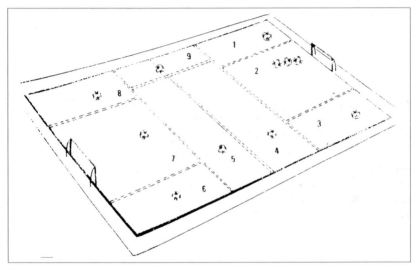

Warm-up

If possible it should take place on another field or else the exercise circuit already set up could be disrupted. Ensure comprehensive warming up takes place. After the warm-up we move to the circuit.

Main part: circuit training
(Three rounds)

First we go with the group from station to station and explain each exercise briefly. Then the players are divided into groups of three. Each group can start where it wants (but only one group per station). In the following we provide an overview of the whole circuit which consists of nine exercises.

Exercise 1: While moving, pass the ball. Pass accurately and hard to the foot. Emphasis: accuracy. Do not tolerate any "standing soccer".

Exercise 2: Goal shot by a midfield player. Player A briefly has the ball and passes to B. The latter passes the ball on to midfield player C. Player B moves off to the right immediately after the pass (to create a gap or to receive the ball). A waits for a possible return pass from C. C shoots at the goal or passes to a fellow player (better: shoot).

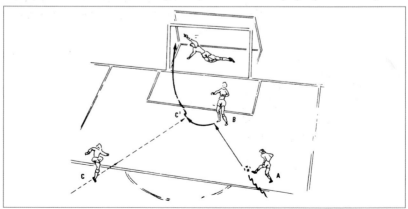

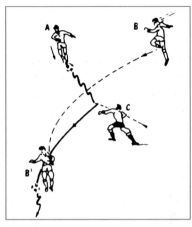

Exercise 3:
By running free players call for a pass into the open space. They run towards the ball at the highest pace possible, the person with the ball quickly plays the ball on (pay attention to the pace of fellow players).

Exercise 4:
Secret play off. Player A plays the ball straight ahead to defender C. Player B runs behind A and gets the ball passed to him "secretly".

Exercise 5: Wall pass (one-two) game. Player A has the ball, plays towards B for a wall pass (one-two). B plays the ball past defender C into the path of A. Emphasis on passing on the ball, running on, playing on and changing pace.

Exercise 6: Bringing a midfield player into the game via the outside line with two options. A plays the ball towards B who gets away from his opposing player with a body feint and receives the pass. B plays directly to C. Then: A dashes to the front, B runs free on the outside line. Player C now plays according to the concrete situation.

Exercise 7: Bringing a midfield player into the game - goal shot. Player A plays the ball, passes to B, who shifts the game to the other side towards player C. The latter plays the ball across towards player A, who is storming up and now closes the attack. Now a variation which can often be used in the game: a player (A) moves up and meets massive opposition. He therefore plays the ball to the wing (B). This player shifts the game to the other side and thus draws the opponents out with him. C (in ball possession) acts as if he is moving out and then suddenly plays towards player A, also suddenly running up, who runs into the path that has been cleared. A shoots to the goal or also passes.

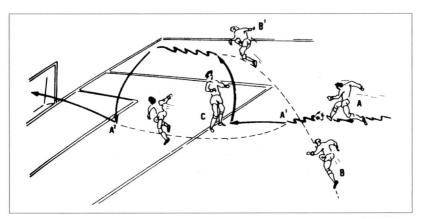

Exercise 8: Bringing a midfield player into the game via the outside line with a following return pass. Player A runs with the ball at his foot towards C. Player B suddenly runs behind player A, and then for his part plays towards C. C lets the ball bounce off B (see Exercise 4). Player A moves up a bit more without getting away from his opposing player. A sticks to the defender. If B wants to kick the pass, A suddenly frees himself, sprints, receives the pass from B

Exercise 9: Heading game with opponent. A player throws the ball and his partner heads the ball back from various positions, despite hindrance by the half active opposing player.

Training Session 13: Fitness Training on the Field

In the meantime we know the exercise sequence in which fitness exercises are carried out right across the field, and the way back is used for recovery (see training session 4 as well): the load can be influenced how the way back is structured. If we let the players walk back, then there is more time for recovery than if we get them to jog back. Then the load is more intensive.

Warm-up

For the warm-up we use a field of 40 m x 40 m. The players form up in 4 rows. A number of exercises which are well suited for the warm-up:

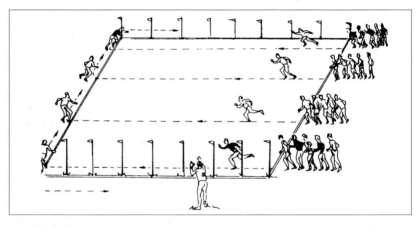

- Circling of arms and shoulders

- Running backwards, turning around halfway and running forwards

- Standing on one leg: circle lower leg and foot

- Running with high knees

- Running sideways, alternately left and right

Main part

The focus is on various forms of movement which turn up in the game again and again, e.g. running, jumping, run/jump, sprints, also with dexterity tasks as well as a number of strength exercises: crawling, carrying etc. We start with a series of five runs across the training field. The first 4 players start. As soon as they have covered 1/3 of the distance, the second group starts etc. so that three groups are always in motion.

Exercise 1: Start at half speed, after 30 m dash over 10 m. In the course of five rounds we systematically shorten the distance which is covered at half speed and increase the distance dashed.

Exercise 2: Easy run over the whole sports field. Now we repeat the previous exercise but start with the long dashes and shorten these after each run.

Exercise 3: After an easy run we come to jumping forms. We run at half speed, at a signal (three times per distance) a jump (simply jump). After this, jump with a header and jump followed by a dash.

Exercise 4: Like Exercise 3, but each time the emphasis is on a high jump (full use of strength).

Exercise 5: To improve mobility and also to now use other muscles, we execute a number of exercises using varying types of forward movement: 10 m exercise, 10 m running, 10 m exercise etc.

Exercise 6: Partner exercises. Each exercise is carried out twice so that the partners can swap roles. A number of examples: horse and rider, wheelbarrow, carrying in front of the chest, carrying on the shoulders, etc.

Exercise 7: After the hard work there is now a winding down phase so that at the end we can start with a series of sharp dashes: at a signal start and dash right to the last metre, come back easily (repeat 5 times).

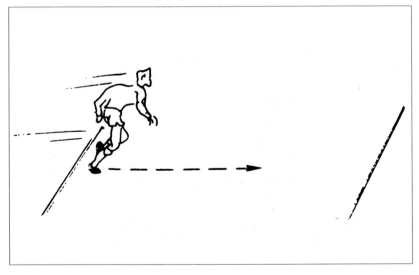

Exercise 8: Starts from varying starting positions:
- Stand with back turned, at a signal turn around and start
- After jumping off with two legs
- From sitting, lying positions
- From a standstill behind the partner
- 5 metres forwards, come back backwards, then sprint

The training is closed with a shuttle relay. Two teams play against each other, half of each team stands on one side of the slalom course, the other half on the other side. At a signal there is a slalom run.
Variants:
a) Accordion run: two poles forwards, one back, 2 forwards etc.;
b) Simple sprints.

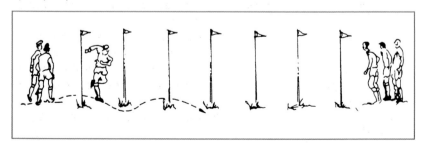

Training Session 14: Special Training for Defence

Originally a special training for defence players was planned for today. All the players asked if they could come, however, because they all - corresponding to our way of playing - also have defence tasks to carry out. The players are right. Furthermore the topic we are covering is important for every player in the midfield: Intercepting an opposing attack. Example: In a certain game situation we have lost the ball in our own attack. Our midfield players had moved up into the attack. I now stand opposite the player who will start the opposing attack. What do I do? Go to the ball or not? Together we discuss a number of basic elements for the defensive game. The last part of the training session consists of a small game in which we concentrate exclusively on proper defence behaviour.

BASIC RULES FOR DEFENDERS
1. Always move between the attacker and your own goal.
2. Always keep your eye on the opponent and the ball.
3. Do not give your opponent room to move.
4. Determine the distance from the opponent.
5. Try to reach the ball before the opponent does (intercept), or, if that is not possible, try to disrupt the opponent's reception of the ball as far as possible (one-on-one, tackling).

6. In your own defence zone avoid dribbles or individually outplaying the opponent. If possible strive for a constructive build-up of the game, but in any case safely play the ball on.

7. On receiving the ball never play the ball inwards (to the own goal). Try to build up further along the outside line. On losing the ball immediately go back between your own goal and the opponent.

8. Avoid uncontrolled passes and clearing kicks. It is better to try to build up an attack with the aid of the midfield.

9. If you are forced to kick the ball away from a dangerous situation, if possible do not kick it forwards into the middle of the field or even worse in front of your own goal. It is better to try to kick the ball to the outside line.

10. On losing the ball or if you have been outplayed, always go back with it, for a team-mate has taken over your position. Therefore, as soon as someone has been outplayed, take over his unoccupied place.

11. Never run towards the person with the ball in too much of a hurry or without thinking, for ... a player who has the ball at his foot is dangerous. If you attack too hard, you will quickly be put out of action and you leave him an unmarked space behind you. It is better to defend by delaying and give your team-mates time to get their bearings.

12. A defender attacks his opponent when he is sure that he can intercept the ball or take it off his opponent in a one-on-one. An opponent with the ball with whom one cannot enter a one-on-one without risk must be held up until support by another defender comes. The opponent's playing space must be blocked.

13. Never attack an opponent in twos. One defender attacks, the second secures the area.

14. In your own penalty area you must keep the angle to your own goal as small as possible. With regard to the available players and their qualities we have chosen a combination of zone and man marking for the season. For pure man marking across the whole playing field mixes up the organisation of defence (changes of position - unoccupied zones). Pure zone marking, on the other hand, is too risky. Therefore we play using zone marking (everyone has their own zone) with man marking for the opponent who comes into the zone.

Under points 11 and 12 we spoke of intercepting an opposing attack by delaying. We have put this rule into a practical training.

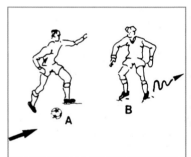

Exercise 1: Situation: We stand opposite a player with the ball carrying out an opposing attack. We do not attack directly, but rather slow the opponent down. Thus the team-mates have time to come back. We are basically a kind of shock absorber in front of the defence. Execution: Player B tries to slow down attacker A - with the ball - by moving back as slowly as possible.

Exercise 2: Game situation: Player A, in ball possession, attacks across the centre. Player B tries to hold him up and to force him into the outer areas which are not a danger to the goal. In doing so, make sure the angle to the goal is well covered.

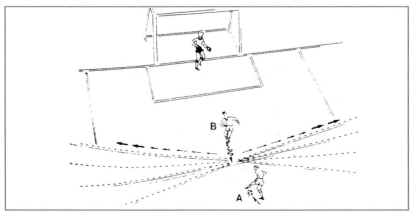

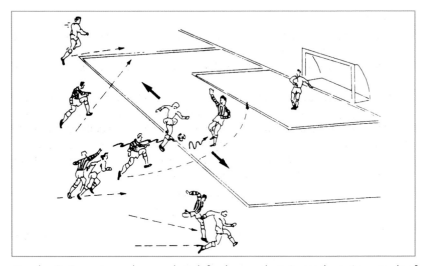

Exercise 3: Game towards a goal: 5 defenders against 4 attackers. As a result of numerical superiority the defence has a man free. This man moves up and attacks the person with the ball. Each time when the direct opponent of the person with the ball has been outplayed, the free defender takes over his task and by using delaying defence tactics tries to allow the outplayed team-mate to return and take over his task again.

Exercise 4: Game: Practising defensive behaviour. The defending team does not directly attack the person with the ball, but rather forms up and applies the 14 previously mentioned basic rules as well as combined zone and man marking.

Training Session 15: Preparatory Game

As a final example for our practical game preparation let us take a home game against an opponent who plays two classes above us (tournament game).

Theoretical preparation

Today's task: We attempt to build up variable attacks from the midfield. The midfield must not be ceded to the opponent. By shifting the game we try to irritate the opponent. We want to keep trying to frequently shoot goals from the second row. The midfield, on the other hand, tries to intercept the attacks of the opponent. For this we always maintain a buffer player in the midfield who plays in front of our defence.

Practical preparation

Defence: Emphasise that the combination of area and man coverage should be used (agreements among each other).

Midfield: Do not do too much with the ball at your feet. Play the ball on in time and run free.

Attack: Take advantage of the opportunities offered without hesitating and courageously go forward. Keep the opponent busy. A very good warm-up is necessary for this difficult game. Begin easily and continually increase the intensity. After the warm-up work with the ball for quite a while and address each player individually. Actively involve the goalkeeper (a number of powerful shots which he can catch relatively easily - encourage him).

Analysis sheet
of the game .... (preparatory game)

Important phases	Central points					Notes/explanations
What moves the game on (ball possession). What stops the opponent's attack (loss of the ball)	1. Good positional play 2. Good execution 3. Intervention 4. Individual game 5. Collective game					
	1	**2**	**3**	**4**	**5**	
Is the ball kept in our own ranks?	Too many get caught up			Waiting and seeing		Game was played too broadly (security). Too little initiative.
Are we playing offensively ?		satisfactory		satisfactory		Attacks too slow Defence sometimes went up, but the midfield was already over-occupied.
Do the midfield/defence move up when the team is in ball possession?	Sometimes				Sometimes	Was often difficult because of the strength and system of the opponent.
Does the "Attack" defend when the ball is lost?	o.K.		Good	o.K.		Disrupted very well and went up with the defenders moving up.
Are the three rows maintained?	o.K.				+ -	Yes, but occasionally let themselves go too long (doubts).
Positional play - individual - collective gone	Yes				1st half	Had to adapt ourselves to the strong opponent little too much.
Is the moving up of the opposing defence made use of?	Yes		Yes			2nd half was even good, good attacks.

Practice game

Basic rule: Shortly before the start of the championships we want to show where we stand.

Task: By playing moving soccer create opportunities and defend in an organised manner.

Post mortem

General assessment

The opponents - playing in a higher class - wanted to qualify for the next round of the tournament. Because of this they developed a kind of "safety first" game, so that the game in the midfield was tough. That was also one of the reasons we were not able to force our game on to the opponents. Surprising actions were only seen rarely.

1st Half

A fairly balanced game. Each team had two goal opportunities. The opponents tried to dominate the midfield from a closed defence but because their game was much too broad in the offensive, often did not get the desired result. As the opponent was at the ball more often than we were, we did not get the game under control. Because of an unnecessary own goal we were down 0:2 after 45 minutes.

2nd Half

For the opponent the game was over. On attack they hardly made use of any opportunities. We got a better look in on the offensive and built up nice attacks which we used for a glorious goal. After that the game got harder because the opponent felt insecure. Our midfield played its defensive role well and the covering tasks were carried out well. Our clever counter actions provided for the necessary agitation.

Training Session 16: Fitness Training - Sprints

Just before the beginning of the championship series we were able to deliver a great game. A difficult game, which we lost by one goal. Exactly for this reason we can analyse the game more realistically and look at it critically. When a game has been won there is usually vain joy and one does not go into the details very much. We will try to maintain the individual and collective strengths and use them in the games ahead of us. On the other hand, our weaknesses show us what our future training tasks must be. We see that there are still many things which need improvement. One problem we must deal with this week is that there are many young players in the 11, side by side with older team mates. In the midfield in particular we cannot imagine being without the exemplary effect and the calming effect of the senior of the team.

Warm-up

As today we have the Cooper Test and a series of acceleration and sprint exercises ahead of us, we make sure of an intensive, comprehensive warm-up without the ball. We work in groups of four. Towards the end we get the players to carry out a number of intensification runs and a series of four sprints.

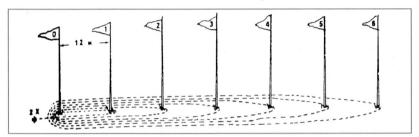

COOPER TEST AND KILOMETRE TEST

After a brief recovery we begin with the Cooper Test. As we know from last time, the idea is to cover as great a distance as possible (around the field) within a period of 12 minutes. It should be a real test which shows where each player stands with regard to his endurance performance ability. Experience shows that the results of a Cooper Test shortly before the season starts are the best. This is because training in this period has been especially for fitness. A distance of 3100 to 3300 metres must be possible. In the following another fitness test, the kilometre test, is introduced: 3-4 players carry out the kilometre test together on a specially prepared course consisting of flagpoles or cones set up 12 metres apart. From the start (0) the players sprint around the first flag pole and back to position 0, from there around the second flagpole etc., until the whole course (500 m) has been covered. Directly afterwards the same course is run a second time. When the players reach position 0 the last time, the time is stopped (followed by poles measurement). The results and the data are noted on a filing card - as with the Cooper Test.

THE KILOMETRE TEST - A FITNESS TEST APPROPRIATE TO SOCCER

The disadvantage of the kilometre test is that it has to be prepared and that only a limited number of players can run at the same time. Nevertheless it is a very good exercise which can be included in fitness training (circuit training). The fitness test and the noting of the results are followed by a phase of active recovery - easily walking, not standing still - during which the players divide themselves into groups of four.

Main part

1. SPRINTS

The players run in groups of four, at a signal they accelerate.

Exercise 1: Accelerations over 10 m (5 times). Stop the times. Afterwards, 45 seconds of recovery.

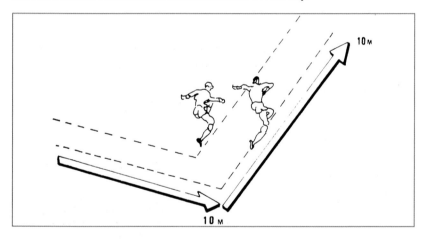

Exercise 2: Sprint over 2 x 10 m, whereby after 10 m (command) dart to the side (90 degree change of direction). 5 times. Afterwards, 25 seconds recovery.

Following the 3 minutes break the series (Exercises 1-3) is repeated. Afterwards 5 minutes break and repeat the series again. Total amount of running: 5 x 10 = 50 + 5 x 20 = 100 + 5 x 30 = 150 x 3 = 900 m. While we prepare the next exercises the players have a break.

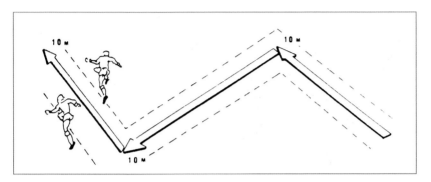

Exercise 3: Sprint over 3 x 10 m, after 10 m in each case (command) change of direction. Five times. Afterwards, 3 minutes break.

2. SLALOM AROUND FLAGPOLES

6 to 9 flagpoles are set up 3 m apart. The players again practise in groups of four (two practise - two recover). Every exercise is carried out twice.

A. Players practise individually
Player 2 starts as soon as Player 1 has reached the last flagpole.

Exercise 1: Sprint to the end - run back easily.

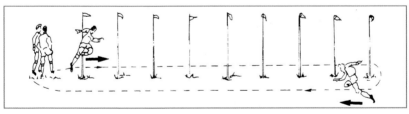

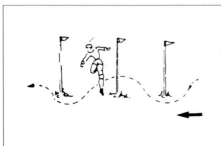

Exercise 2: Slalom run

Exercise 3: Run around the flagpole - accelerations between the poles - run carefully round the flagpole.
Exercise 4: Run around the poles - easy slalom around two poles - sprint around the poles.

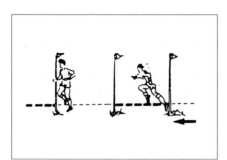

Exercise 5: Sprint - trot - sprint etc - from pole to pole in each case .

Exercise 6: Accordion run. Run forwards around 2 poles - backwards around one pole, 2 forwards etc.

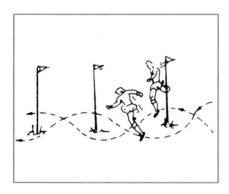

B. Players practise in pairs
As soon as one pair has reached the last flagpole, the second pair starts. The first pair trot back easily.
Exercise 1: The person running ahead increases and slows his pace at every second pole. The second man follows as closely as possible.
Exercise 2: Slalom around poles, the paths of the players cross.

Exercise 3: Slalom run at full speed. The second man follows as closely as possible.
Exercise 4: Slalom, players run behind each other. At each pole the second person overtakes the one in front.

C. Players practise in threes
The moment they return to the starting position the last man drops out and another player joins in.

Exercise 1: Run sideways in slalom around the poles. Always face towards the pole.
Exercise 2: Slalom around the poles; at each pole the person in front drops back and closes up behind.
Exercise 3: Take over leadership: After a pole has been run around, the last man goes to the front in order to run around the next pole first.

RECOVERY
Now that everyone has had enough of running, let them play: 6 versus 6 on half a playing field. The only condition: accurate passes.

Training Session 17: Station Training

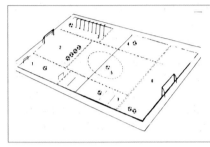

For today we have worked out a fairly load intensive training using stations. The advantages of such a training are that none of the players can get out of a particular form of load, the players can work in small groups and with a regular sequence of exercises. The coach can determine the training objective through the exercises he chooses. If you want to carry out fitness training, then that is possible both with and without the ball. It is also possible to include specific elements of the soccer game. A further positive aspect is the total inclusion of the reserve players. It does happen sometimes that these players are left to themselves on the side of the field while

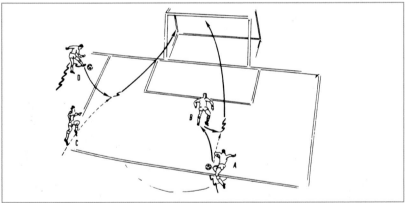

the trainer works with the core. As a result they can feel somewhat neglected. For today we have developed a diverse fitness training, mostly with the ball. It is up to the trainer to determine the loads: the higher the pace, the greater load.

Warm-up

The players practise in pairs. Because the training stations have already been prepared, we carry out the warm-up next to the field.

Main part

We divide the players into groups of four and then briefly explain the exercises. At each station they practise five minutes. At the end, at a command they gather up the material and slowly go to the next exercise station. The station course is completed twice in a row, the second time there is more emphasis on speed.

Exercise 1: Roll ball, two against two. The ball may only be played with the hands and must stay on the ground. In other words, do not throw it. Two small goals 1 m wide, about 20 m apart.

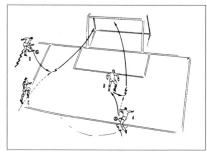

Exercise 2: Goal shot training in pairs. Options: a) accurate pass into the path of the team-mate and shot at goal, b) wall pass – goal shot.

Exercise 3: Two players stand before a row of flagpoles, the two others about 7 m behind the last pole, whereby the distance between these two is also about 7 m. Player A has the ball. Player C starts and runs in a slalom around the poles. At the last pole he heads the ball thrown him by player A to B. Now B starts, player A runs to the starting point, player B takes up the position of A with the ball and C takes up the position of B.

Exercise 4: Wrestling ring. The four players link hands to form a circle around the ball. They try to force one of the fellow players to touch the ball.

Exercise 5: Party ball game two against two. Emphases: Running free and passing the ball. Each pair counts the successful passes in sequence.

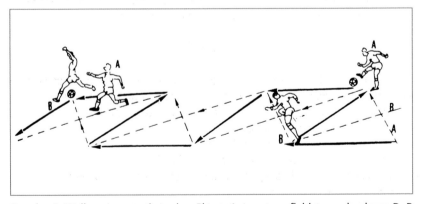

Exercise 6: Wall pass game in series. Player A passes upfield towards player B. B sprints diagonally to meet the pass and passes across the breadth to A, who in turn sprints in diagonally. Continuously. At the end of the field they exchange positions.

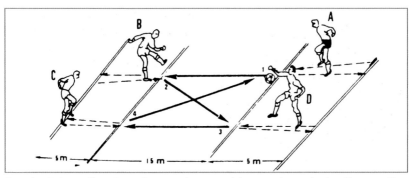

Exercise 7: Accordion. Four players take up positions as shown in the diagram. Run in towards the pass and back again. At speed.

Training Session 18: Special Training for the Mid-field

What was originally meant to be a special training for the midfield players was changed to a general training by the team squad with the reasoning: "Coach, in the game we also have to be able to do everything: attack, defend etc., so we also want to learn as much as possible." Therefore we have developed a training session which, in addition to a theoretical discussion of midfield play also involves putting certain strategies into practice in standard situations.

Considerations regarding midfield play

First we take stock of the situation together with the players with regard to a number of terms and thoughts expressed by the players about the midfield.

- Long passes look good and are also dangerous for the opponent, but they are often inaccurate and hard to receive.
- We must build up the game from the midfield.
- In an attack support must come from the midfield.
- The midfield must really shape the game variably, and then a long pass is certainly all right as a variation.
- The midfield should not only build up the game, but also take on defence tasks when the ball is lost.
- What must we do when we are in possession and what when the ball is lost?

- A game maker, i.e. a switching station which can be played to as often as possible, would be an advantage.

Using these thoughts and remarks of the players, the coach can give the players a certain insight into the role of the midfield, without claiming to cover everything.

Functions of the midfield: attack

In the midfield you have the best creative options - both to attack and to defend. But... you have to work very hard there and it is a role which is not always obvious. The quality and the playing system of a team are dependent above all on the defence qualities of the eleven. This does not mean that you should just play defensively, but it is a fact we must be aware of. Let us start with the attack actions. Attack actions take place when you are in possession of the ball. Following are some characteristic functions of the midfield when in possession:

- Build up and prepare the attack
- Game without the ball.
- Do not keep the ball too long, but combine.
- Let the ball go: the ball never gets tired - in contrast to the players.
- The closing pass (deep, broad, cross) - e.g. long pass into the open space or short cross into the back of a defender.
- Shift the game - create free spaces.
- Surprisingly push through without the ball - support during attack.
- Teamwork with the forwards - e.g. on the wings: winger moves in, midfield player moves up into the free space left by him.
- Move up yourself - sudden attack or initiative for a wall-pass with a forward.
- Goal shots from the second row.
- When the opponent uses the off side trap - pass to player coming from the second row, or place the ball in front of yourself when the opponents move up in a line.
- Intercepting balls passed back - pass or (even better), if possible, goal shot.

Functions of the midfield: defence

The chosen playing system stands and falls with the defence qualities of the team, especially in the midfield. Therefore we will examine these situations carefully. Each of the following points could be the subject of a training session on the field. Let's face it, most training exercises are for the offensive. It is also more difficult to develop enjoyable and sensible training exercises which focus on defence behaviour. Do not make it too complicated; try to explain in the theory part what you intend and practise this in the training on the playing field in a clear and simple way. First practise a game situation with one player, and then gradually add further players. In this way try to put together a defence block. Defence actions take place when the ball is lost. We want to prevent the opponent from playing and shooting goals. The following are some defence functions of the midfield:

- Commitment - also (and especially) when the ball is lost.
- If the opponent has the ball the midfield must jointly form a line of defence in front of their own defenders. Each player must have his responsibilities and know them well so that the defence is not suddenly confronted by a numerical superiority of the opponent.
- Move back as quickly as possible and take over covering responsibilities.
- Create a buffer in front of the defence - hold up the opponent.
- Each covers an opponent in the midfield as quickly as possible.
- Do not let any opponent move up unmarked - go with them. This also applies, and to no small degree, to the forwards.
- Right after losing the ball the opposing game maker in particular must be deactivated.
- If you are confronted alone by an opponent with the ball and your team-mates have not yet come back, carefully attack the opponent and try to force him outwards. Once everyone is in position and coverage is assured, attack powerfully and full of conviction to get the ball back.
- Do not let the opponent play in the midfield because that is where he builds the game up, just as we do.
- Go with an opponent who runs into free spaces.

Exercises: standard situations

After this somewhat dry but necessary theory we loosen up today's training with some exercises derived from standard situations. These include free kicks and corner kicks. A free kick gives us certain advantages. It is worth working out various alternatives for these situations. Using what we are capable of as a starting point, in the case of a free kick we can create a game situation which gives us a chance to score. Make the effort to work out solutions in detail, motivate the players to do the same and avoid improvisations. What facts can we assume when developing a free kick? The following is always given:

- The position of the ball,
- The distance from the opposing goal,
- The way the free kick may be shot (directly or - indirectly).

Before that we can determine:

- The place our own players will take up,

- The way we execute the free kick,
- Deceptive actions we want to use.

After theoretically working out a number of options we choose predestined players. With them we go through all phases carefully. The other players play a game three against three on another part of the field. In the previous year the following free kick variant led to 6 goals, but it can only be used once against any one opponent (the second time execute this free kick the other way round). Good preparation is necessary, but the players have fun learning these variants.

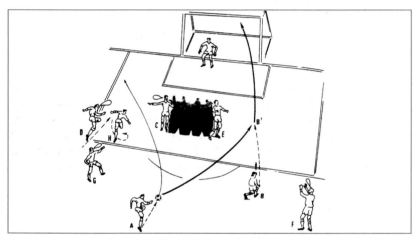

Exercise 1: Indirect free kick. We need 7 to 8 players of whom two are directly involved in execution while the other 6 distract the opponents. As player B - main person - we choose a player who can shoot at goal well while running and who can "act" well.

Execution: Whistle for free kick. Player B rushes up quickly to put the ball in place as he announces that he will take the free kick. Player A takes the ball off him saying: "You want to do everything here, get out of it". Then B really goes to town, curses everyone and everything, goes back to his place "discouraged", signals with his arm "forget about me, you can all drop dead", and plays around with his bootlaces (in their starting positions C-D-G-H discuss - within hearing of the opponents - how they will execute the free kick (D asks C to play the ball "there" and C "innocently" points to where the ball will be played). H and G create a disturbance. E leans uninterestedly against the wall, and nobody even looks at B. As A looks as though he is about to shoot, F says to B something like: "Don't be so stupid", or "If you don't want to play any more, then get off the field", etc. Now the noise for the distracting manoeuvre is at its greatest and A passes - accurately to the agreed spot - while B starts off quickly and shoots.

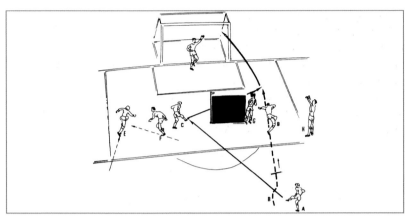

Exercise 2: Direct free kick. Stepping-over-the-ball - as a feint - can also be used very well with the necessary distracting manoeuvres. Here 6 players are involved: 3 carrying it out and three "comedians". First H calls for the ball. B pretends to start and immediately or with some delay A plays to C. At the same time E and F sprint behind C (careful of offside) and call for the ball. Player C does not jump over the ball, but rather plays on to B (G keeps the wall back) who shoots.

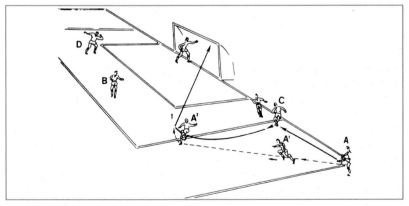

Exercise 3: Short corner. A corner played short can be a good idea especially when you are dealing with an opponent who is very good at heading. As in the last exercise the ball is called for at the second post. The short pass can always be played because the opponent must always be at least 9 m away from the ball. If B starts off surprisingly, then he usually has no direct opponent. Player C moves the ball sideways in front of player A who, coming from the corner, sprints through and shoots towards the short corner. The other players get out of the trajectory,

but in such a way that players B and D always lie in wait of defended balls. If the path is clear and player A is concentrated, there is a real chance of scoring. It is important that the whole thing is well practised.

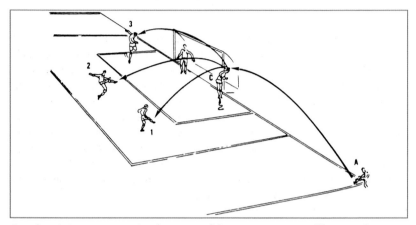

Exercise 4: Long corner. In the case of long corners we adhere to the same principle: agreed positions and some players who irritate the opponent. Example: Corner towards the first post. The disturbance naturally moves to the second post where the ball is called for. It is agreed to whom player C will pass the ball on to (to the side or head on further backwards). In the latter case the centre of unrest is naturally shifted to another place. The team-mates draw the opponent away from the place where the ball is to be played to. And the player who is to receive the ball hides his intentions as long as possible.

13 Soccer-specific Training (High Season)

Training Session 19: Change of Pace

To increase the thrust of attacks from the midfield we teach the players some basic rules of changing pace. An individual change of pace can involve suddenly moving in deep to open an attack or moving up to support an attack. A collective change of pace consists of a series of sudden changes of pace and direction (crossing - passing on the ball). Therefore the emphasis is on the physical aspect and the collective change of pace. One of the most effective tactical means in an attack is playing without the ball. Playing without the ball is not only sprinting in deep but is a real piece of teamwork which the players must safely master in order to use it in the game. It is of course not possible to apply this tool during the entire game, but it can be decisive in the moment when you think you can get the upper hand. A collective change of pace does not mean
• high playing pace of the whole team
• forcing up the pace
• collectively storming the goal.
These three situations can be blocked by the opponent because they are predictable. A collective change of pace is a sudden sequential exploding of various players according to the motto: Running free is better than standing free. (The degree of your effectiveness will depend on your qualities. The change of pace of an individual player is already risky.) If, however, we know how to use this collectively, we have already made good progress. Changes of pace must be well trained. Training on the field will certainly be hard, but the coach does not do this in order to "wear out" the players. All exercises are always only a means to reach our objective. (It will be hard for you sometimes. But each week it will be harder for the opponents if we know how to use the weapon of changing our pace.)

Warm-up

A fairly extensive warm-up. Today up we provide another example of a warm-up without the ball. In the following training sessions we will give a few examples of warm-ups with the ball. We work in two rows in snaking lines across the width of the field.
• Run easily, alternately raising the right and left thigh.
• Run easily, striking heels against buttocks.
• Walk easily, circling the arms, alternately forwards and backwards.

- Run easily, every five steps draw the feet together, knee bends and spring back twice.
- Adjusted steps: five left, five right.
- Run sideways, left and right.
- Walk, at every third step swing up stretched right leg to outstretched left hand (alternately right and left).
- Walk five steps, forward bends, let the arms dangle, then five steps and simultaneously stretch the arms up (at each step stretch the arms up).
- Run easily, at a signal jump (5 times).
- Walk, circling the torso, to the left and to the right.
- Walk, swinging the legs apart forwards, upwards, sideways.
- Walk, overtake the person in front up with a change of pace (in snake lines).
- Walk, walk quickly, constantly overtake the person in front.
- Increase pace, body feint, sprint past the person in front, easily trot on, (continuously until the end of the field).
- In snake lines overtake each other, systematically increase speed.
- In snake lines overtake each other, at speed.

Exercise 1

Main part

After the warm-up we maintain the formation in two lines and work another 15 minutes in snaking lines. The second line sprints past the first and reduces the pace, then this is repeated.

Exercise 1: Both lines run forwards as usual, doing the following:
a) Emphasise starting speed and acceleration (then gradually slow down),
b) Increase the pace and suddenly sprint past the person in front,
c) Begin at half speed and increase the pace at every repetition,
d) Execute a body feint just in the moment before overtaking the person in front (feint left and overtake on the right, and vice-versa).

Exercise 2: As above, but now the first man runs backwards, turns around and chases the player who runs past him and then also begins to run backwards. Repeat exercises a) to d).

Exercise 2

Exercise 3   *Exercise 4*

Exercise 3: As exercises a) to d), but now both players run backwards. The second man turns around before accelerating, dashes, turns around again, and the partner follows in the same way. The emphasis is on sudden, fast turning.

Exercise 4: We maintain the two lines, but give up the snaking lines. Interval: Sprint 10 m, recover, sprint over the width of the field, come back easily (4 times).

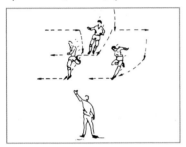

Exercise 5   *Exercise 7*

Exercise 5: The coach stands 20 m away from the players and gets them to briefly accelerate in the direction indicated (5 m, then slow down). Forwards, left, right, backwards, with a jump (point up). Insert a very intensive resting break off two minutes and repeat.

Exercise 6: Two lines practise across the width of the field. Start easily and increase the pace every 10 metres in order to reach maximum speed over the last 10 metres. Make sure sprinting is right to the very last metre.

Exercise 6

Exercise 7: Individual change of pace, in pairs. For 30 seconds the leader tries to shake off the pursuer with changes of pace and direction. The pursuer reacts as quickly as possible. Short break (each player runs in front three times).

COLLECTIVE CHANGE OF PACE

The players work in groups of six, from the centre line to the goal line up (three groups run to one side, three groups to the other), trot easily back to the centre.

Exercise 1: Start easily, one after the other the groups sprint 10 m. Repeat, but now the second group follows the first and the third the second more closely and quickly. Finish: As closely and quickly as possible.

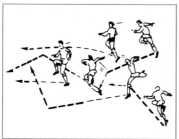

Exercise 2: The same principle, but now intersect from alternating sides. Repeat, but now in shorter and faster sequence. Finish: Each player dashes in a direction which he determines himself; call and mutually encourage each other to sprint.

Exercise 3: Repeat the previous exercises with the same groups, but now with the ball. At a slower pace. Look for gaps and free areas, call for the ball. As soon as everything is moving quickly, emphasis on change of pace. Afterwards emphasis on running in different directions.

Exercise 4: Rows of six. One after the other each player takes over leadership for 1 minute. Then he goes back to the last place. The others follow each other at a distance of 10 metres. The leader determines the direction.

Training Session 20: Stations with the Ball

The big moment is getting closer. For this reason, before the final training session we prepare the players tactically for the first points game on Sunday. We discuss the distribution of responsibilities and cover some special points. The reserves should not be forgotten. We have developed an appropriate training in which the ball is always at the centre of attention:

• Warm-up with the ball on the playing field,
• Stations using the ball,
• Repetition of a number of automatisms,
• Practising of throw-ins,
• Game.

Warm-up

The players form up on the four sides of the playing field. Half of the players have a ball. Two lines standing opposite start off at the same time. At the halfway point the ball is taken over. On reaching the opposite side the other two lines start.

• Moving with the ball (3 times across the field).
• The same, but now alternately play the ball from the right to the left foot.
• The same, but now with small changes of direction.
• The same, now with changes of pace (3 times across the field).
• Moving the ball, take up the ball and throw it high, get the ball under control with the foot, continuously (twice across the field).
• Moving the ball, run around the ball and move it on again.
• Walk with the ball, circling the ball around your body.
• Kick the ball 3 m forwards, run after it with high knees.
• Run, rolling the ball with one hand.
• Run backwards, draw the ball with you alternately using the left and right foot.
• Move the ball at high speed across the field four times.

Main part

STATIONS

In order to carry out a number of important exercises in a short time and without losing too much time we have developed eight practice stations for groups of three. In some groups the goalkeeper can join in the whole time. You know the drill: Players practise at each station for 4 minutes and then go to the next one. After the hard fitness training on Tuesday, the focus is now on accuracy.

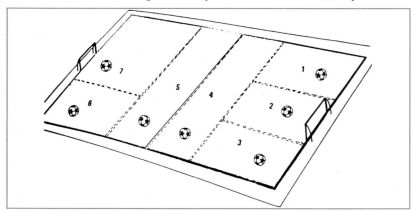

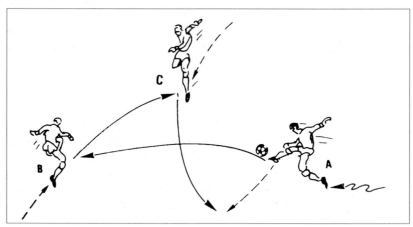

Exercise 1: Pass in front of a running player. Play the pass fairly hard to your team-mate. Get the ball under control and carry on playing. All players are constantly in motion and offer themselves.

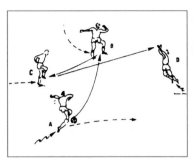

Exercise 2: The same exercise, but now the ball is played directly. The players make sure they can always be played to by running to more favourable positions.

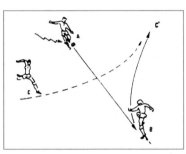

Exercise 3: The same exercise, but now the emphasis is on the third man's playing without the ball. A moves the ball. At the moment when Player B is to be played to, C already decides on the place where he will be played to by Player B. Player C of course hides his intention as long as possible. Regularly change responsibilities.

Exercise 4: Automatise tactical behaviour: Shield ball and pass it on to a team-mate. B moves the ball in the direction of A. At the last moment B simply leaves the ball standing for A. Then B sprints away and receives a pass from A.

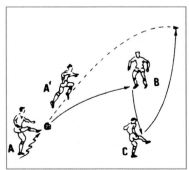

Exercise 5: Attack combination in threes: Support from the second row. Midfield player A plays to forward B who, however, is covered. B plays back to team-mate C who plays behind B towards A, who has meanwhile sprinted into the depth of the field.

Exercise 6: Two against one. By using clean passing play take advantage of numerical superiority. Play wall passes/wall pass/one-twos.

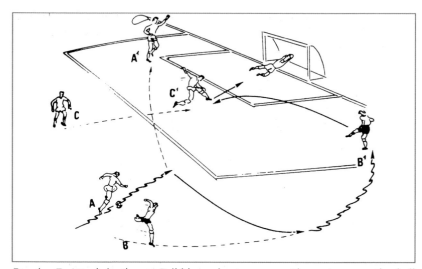

Exercise 7: Attack in threes: Dribble and return pass. Player A moves the ball towards the inside. Team-mate B receives the pass and dribbles to the goal line. A has meanwhile sprinted through and calls for the ball on the other side, but B moves the ball in front of C, who suddenly dashes off, after behaving "passively" (hide your intention as long as possible and dash off at the last moment).

Throw-in 1

THROW-IN EXERCISES

Throw-in 1: Long throw-in in front of the goal. First a short throw-in is feigned (Player B calls and offers himself), player A throws towards C and D running in.

Throw-in 2: Throw-in to forward coming back. Forward B comes back (defender is drawn with him) and calls for the ball. Player C dashes into the free area and receives the throw-in from A.

Throw-in 2

Throw-in 3

Throw-in 3: Throw-in with shifting of the game. Normally when there is a throw-in there is a gathering of players. In order to shift the game at the throw-in, player A throws the ball towards B, who then

- can play the ball back to A who plays the ball into the centre where C and D are standing ready,
- kicks the ball directly to the centre himself with an overhead kick.

GAME

Two teams play against each other. The coach actively follows play. Ensure there is not too much physical involvement. Let the ball run. After the game carry out a number of loosening exercises.

Training Session 21: Fitness Training in Fixed Station Training

After the first - successful - baptism of fire in points games we now have the opportunity to assess the team under competition conditions. What seems important is the fact that - apart from tactical preparation in the changing room -, massaging the players before the warm-up had a psychologically positive effect on them. Although physiologically the massage is only of limited value, you can use the special atmosphere to talk to the players. A masseur who tells the player that his muscles are all right and that the player is fit creates a good basis for the coach who can build on this in the warm-up. We will cover a few tactical weaknesses, e.g. hitting a cross, in our Thursday training session. Today we will carry out fitness training in alternating teams.

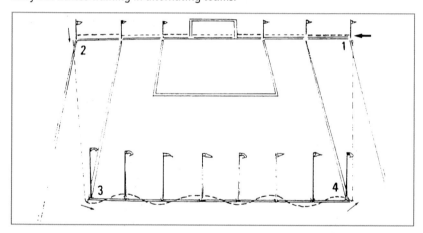

Warm-up

We carry out the warm-up with the entire group on the prepared field. Start very easily and step up gradually.

Main part

We divide the players into groups of six. Because six players would be too many at the first station, there we again divide into 2 groups. For the other groups we mark the second practising area. A station must not necessarily be marked with flagpoles. You can also use the marking lines.

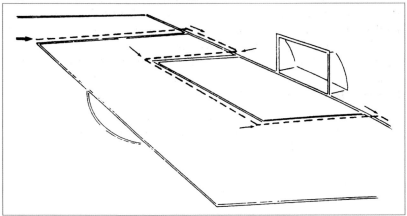

FIRST STATION

Here the players independently carry out an interval programme: Walking - sprinting; trotting easily - sprint with tasks to make it more difficult. This station offers many possibilities. Some examples:
- Slalom around the poles
- Double slalom
- Run around each pole
- Sprint forwards, brake at the pole, go back backwards, brake at the pole, trot forwards to the next pole and then sprint etc.
- Walk, then sprint from one pole to the next
- Run, feint before the pole, run closely past it (continuous)
- Run, 360 degree turn around the pole and then sprint
- Run, carry out a jump at every pole; in doing so you can emphasise the kind of jump (alternately left, right and with both legs), the jump itself or a header at the right moment.

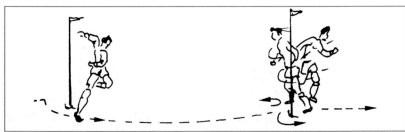

The players practise for about 15 minutes, then swap with the players on the second station. When these players come back again after 15 minutes, we get them to work in pairs. This stimulates their will to perform. Finally the players practise in groups of three.

SECOND STATION

At this station mainly strength exercises are carried out. The players again practise in groups of six. After two carrying or jumping exercises each, insert a running exercise, e.g. "follow-my-leader". During the carrying exercises the players can swap roles freely. Some possibilities:

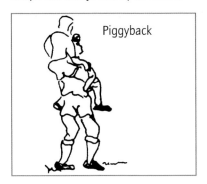
Piggyback

Leapfrog

Follow-my-leader

Two carry one (cradle)

Training Session 22: Training in Game Form

Do not be led astray by the word game. Training in game form can be very demanding physically because the competitive spirit and striving to perform of the players is addressed. Everyone wants to win of course.
The content of the two following examples is:
1. Increase the pace when passing on the ball
2. See and play when the game is shifted.
Both games can be carried out parallel. On a marked field of 20 m x 10 m we play soccer tennis, on the other half of the field we organise a game.

Soccer tennis

Organisation: 5 against 5 on a field 20 m x 10 m, which is divided in half by a net or a rope. Game rules as in volleyball: In each phase of the game the team may touch the ball three times - not more than once per player. On reaching five points the losing team runs once around the field. When they get back, change sides.

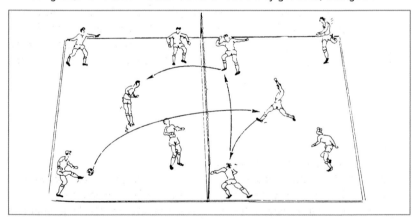

Variant 1: The ball may touch the ground once between two contacts. The ball may be freely played with the foot, knee or head.

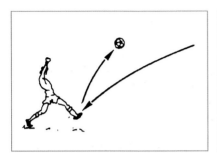 

Variant 2:
The ball may be played freely but may not touch the ground between the three contacts.

Variant 3:
The ball may only be played with the head. The rule about touching the ground does not apply.

Variant 4: The three previous variants can be repeated while making them considerably more difficult: immediately after playing the ball the player sprints to the outside line where he must touch an object (ball) before coming back into the game.

Competition - Broad game

Prerequisites: 2 small goals (1 m wide) and 2 poles.
The diagram shows the formation and the way of playing. The objective is to make use of the possibility of shifting the game to confuse the opponents.
Game content: Team B plays without a goalkeeper towards the large goal and defends the two small goals on the sidelines. Team A plays with a goalkeeper and defends the large goal. They attack the small goals with the handicap that during every attack they have to play past the flagpole furthest away from the goal. If they are playing towards the left goal, then they play around the right flagpole and vice versa. Once the flagpole in question has been played around, however, then shifting the game to the other goal (wall pass/wall pass/one-two across wide) is allowed. This also excludes "taking up position" before an opponent's goal. The coach observes the game and gets the teams to swap roles after 10 minutes. After 20 minutes they swap with the first playing group.

Training Session 23: Fitness Training in Groups of Six

An interesting variant of fitness training is to let various groups compete against each other in a kind of competition. We devise various playful competition forms in which the groups can play against each other, and award points. You will be astonished at how much the players of the individual groups exert themselves in order to help their group get points. In a playful way we thus encourage a number of things such as:
- The commitment of the individual players
- Commitment for the team
- Attention in the game
- Reaction capability under load
- Independent working of a group as a result of self-motivation

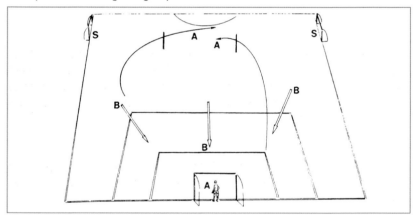

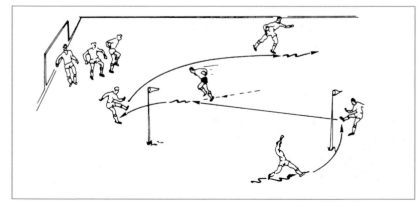

As mentioned, in order to maintain excitement we award points. Prepare a sheet on which you write down the groups horizontally across the top and on the left vertically the numbers of the exercises. The first group gets e.g. 3 points, the second 2 and the third group 1. Between each series and after the last series there is always active recovery in the form of a small game. Players can move about freely and the coach has time to prepare the next exercises. Today we choose "horse soccer" to fill the breaks. In each case six play against six, four minutes long (3 x horse and rider against 3 x horse and rider). Instead of soccer, "horse handball" can be played.

Main part

After an intensive warm-up we can begin with the first exercise series. In order to keep the whole thing as simple as possible, we choose exercises in which we can always use the prepared running course of 20 m. Mark the start and turning points with a flagpole or a cone. Each exercise is carried out three times. Each series consists of five exercises.

SERIES 1
For each group we need a medicine ball and a weight vest. The six players form up at the starting line. The first one runs, sends the next person off and closes up at the back again (three times).

Exercise 1: Dash to the turning-point and back.

SERIES 2

The coach has noted the points and the first horse soccer game is over. The second series takes place on the same course but now the players take up position on the running course. At a signal player 1 starts and runs through the slalom course until he is back at his place. Then he calls and player 2 can start etc. (three times).

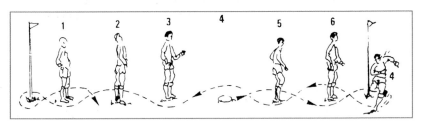

Exercise 1: Slalom through the player rows to the turning point, slalom back to the second turning point and slalom back to the starting point.

Exercise 2:
The same exercise but now run around each player.

Exercise 3:
The same exercise, but now go between their legs.

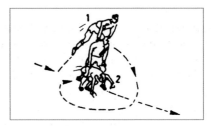

Exercise 4:
The same exercise, but now leap frogging.

Exercise 5:
Leapfrog over each player (1), go back and then between the legs of the same player (2).

SERIES 3

For this exercise we use our prepared running course for the last time, three players form up behind each turning point. In order to increase the pace the players now only run one length, therefore we need two medicine balls per group.

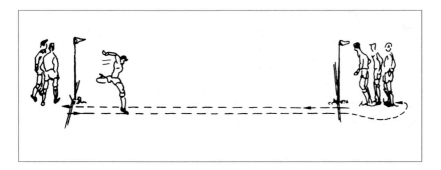

Exercise 1: At a signal the first player runs to the other side, tags the first person; he runs off, the other player closes up behind.

SERIES 4
For the last game the players form a circle with a diameter of 20 metres. Five players stand on the circle line, the sixth in the centre. Each group has a medicine ball.

Exercise 2: Sprint, jump over two medicine balls.
Exercise 3: Carry the medicine ball and hand it over.
Exercise 4: Carry the medicine ball to the middle, call, then the first man on the other side starts, takes over the ball and returns.
Exercise 5: Kick a medicine ball forwards with your foot to the other side.

Exercise 1: Player 1 starts with a medicine ball and gives this to player 6 (in the centre). Player 6 sprints to player 2 while player 1 stays in the centre. Changeover of players 2 and 6 etc. (three times).

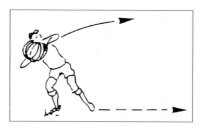

Exercise 2:
The same exercise, but now the medicine ball is rolled forwards with one foot.

Exercise 3:
The same exercise, but throw the ball (or roll it) and run after it.

Exercise 4:
The same exercise, but run backwards carrying the ball.

Exercise 5:
The same exercise, but run forwards with the ball on your neck.

Training Session 24: Fitness Training with the Ball

In this fitness training session the emphasis is on speed ability and speed of execution. The warm-up is also aimed at this. We need one ball per player for this. If there are not enough balls, players can practise in pairs or threes.

Warm-up

The players practise in 2 lines across the width of the field.
• Move the ball running easily.
• Run easily, moving the ball alternately with the right and left foot.
• Easily run with the ball in your hand, at a signal knee-bends, bouncing back, arms held forwards.
• Move the ball running easily. At a signal stop the ball with the sole of the foot.

- Roll the ball with your hands.
- Run easily, move the ball and alternately shield the ball to the left and right.
- While running throw the ball up high and catch it jumping.
- Move the ball with changes of pace.
- Pin the ball between your feet and hop, at a signal do a sideways straddle and pass the ball around your spread legs in such a way that its course is like a figure of eight.
- Run with the ball at your feet, pass it over 10 m and dash after it.
- Dribble with changes of pace and direction.
- At speed: run with the ball at your feet.

Main part

We divide the players into groups of six which are further divided into three pairs with a ball each. The other balls are put to the side. Never leave material on the field which is not needed as this distracts the players (kicking away balls etc.).

There now follows a series of exercises which can be carried out in pairs along the length of the field. Each exercise is carried out four times so that the total running distance is about 2800 m. On one side one pair forms up, on the starting side the other four players stand. The first pair (1) (on the starting side) carries out the exercise along the length of the field and is relieved by pair 2 etc.

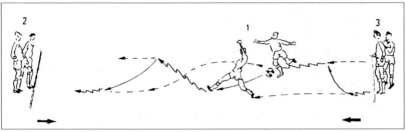

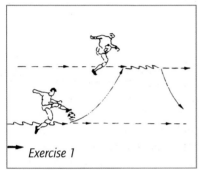

Exercise 1

Exercise 1: The partners form up about 7 m apart and play each other the ball kicking it into their partner's path. Begin slowly and systematically increase the pace. Make sure passes are clean.

Exercise 2: Player A stands 7 m from B. Start: A runs backwards and B runs forwards with the ball. B plays the ball to A who, running backwards, passes the ball back each time. Alternately hard and soft passes.

Exercise 2

Exercise 3: Running with changes of direction. Player A - together with player B, about 7 m from him - dribbles, followed by B, the ball into the depth of the field. With the ball at his feet, A crosses the running direction of B, while B sprints obliquely behind him, as he does so A passes the ball into his path.

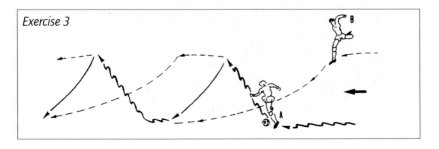

Exercise 3

Exercise 4

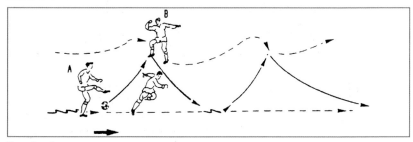

Exercise 5

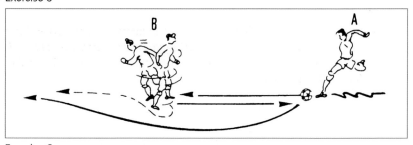

Exercise 6

Exercise 4: Position and movement as in Exercise 2. Running backwards, A plays the ball to B who acts as though he will play the ball back (carry out the feint in an exaggerated way), but then lets the ball go, turns around briefly and with a dash gets the ball under control. Ball back to A and repeat.

Exercise 5: Wall pass. Position and running directions as in Exercise 1. Now A plays a wall pass with Player B each time - who follows at a sprint .

Exercise 6: Play off and run on. This exercise is a combination of exercises 2 and 4. Player A passes to player B while running, B gives the ball back. A then puts the ball past B who turns around and sprints after him with the ball.

Exercise 7: Make room. Both players run forwards on a line, A about 7 m in front of B who is in ball possession. Suddenly B takes off at speed, player A accelerates sideways just as suddenly and calls for the ball. Now B, with the ball at his feet, increases to maximum speed.

GAME

To finish we get the players to play a game on the small field (30 m x 20 m) "with reversed goals". This means only goals scored from behind count. The game will develop on its own in such a way that passes are played across the width behind the goal or the ball is centred.

Training Session 25: Fitness Training with a Skipping Rope

The skipping rope not only offers a welcome change in fitness training, it also particularly develops jumping strength and coordination ability. In addition, heart and lung functions are improved by the intensive exercise. Each player is given a rope. If we are working on a playing field, one rope for two players is also sufficient; the first and second line with ropes, one row without a rope etc. On coming back the ropes are handed over. It is neither necessary nor a good idea to carry out the complete training with skipping ropes. The coach must always make sure that the players do not suffer training, but really experience it and the latter can only be achieved by a making training full of diversity. The exercises take place on a field 25 x 10 m. Players form up in four rows next to each other, with a leader on the right. To help them get used to the course, but even more so to the skipping rope, we get the players to do the course three or four times at an easy pace.

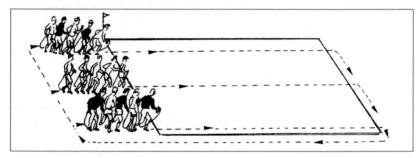

Warm-up

• Skipping rope strokes with slightly jumping running steps.
• Skipping while hopping on the spot.

• Run easily forwards, but swing the rope backwards.
• Closing hop with skipping strokes forwards (5 times), trot 5 steps, then repeat.

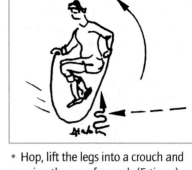

- Double up the rope, swing it in a circle and jump over it.

- Hop, lift the legs into a crouch and swing the rope forwards (5 times) and repeat.
- Run easily with skipping strokes.

- The doubled up rope is taken in one hand. At elbow height swing the rope in a semi-circle to the left and right.
- The same exercise, but with the rope stretched in both hands, follow the course of the rope with your eyes.

- Running easily swing the doubled up rope over your head, alternately with the left and right hand.

• Skipping while running backwards.

• Hold the rope tight at one end and drag it along the ground between your legs.
• a) Bending forward look towards the end of the rope.
• b) Alternately turn your upper body to the left and right and look towards the end of the rope.

Main part

• Forward skipping strokes while running, increasing the pace.
• Forward skipping strokes while running, at every third step jump up.
• Forward skipping strokes while running, at every third step knee bends and then a stretch jump over the rope.

- Fold up the rope four times and while walking hold it up and move it down.
- Fold the rope four times in both hands Jump over the rope.
- Take the rope folded into four in both hands. With outstretched arms wide circling of your torso.

- Stand on the rope with both feet and hop forwards (pulling the rope).
- The same exercise but at every third step jump as high as possible (pull powerfully).

- Exercise in pairs: Players A and B stand 10 m apart. One player practises, the other recovers. Player A runs one round skipping until he reaches the starting point again. Then player B starts. Who can run the round fastest? Various obstacles can be included or a team competition carried out.

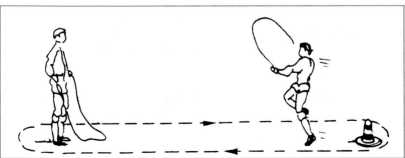

EXERCISES TO PERFECT BALL CONTROL AND GOAL SHOOTING

4 balls for each exercise. The pace is increased somewhat each time.

Exercise 1: 4 balls lie in front of the first pole, slalom around the poles and shoot at goal.

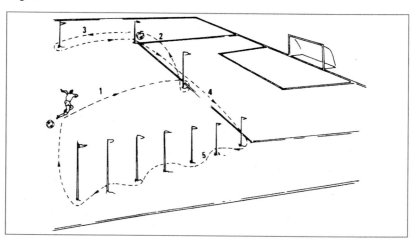

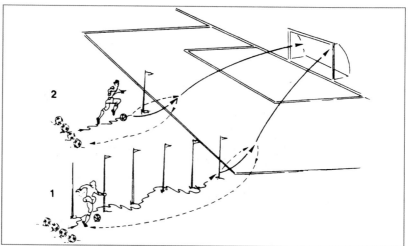

Exercise 2: Play around the pole, before the shot place your standing leg properly and shoot at the goal.

Exercise 3: The coach throws the ball to the player, the player runs past the ball, turns and shoots at goal.

Training Session 27: Fitness Training

Because we need a number of balls for the second section of training we can already include these balls in the warm-up. It may sound simple, but the balls on the playing field give the players a lift even when these balls are not being used directly. We place these balls in two rows (6 to 7 metres apart) so that for the warm-up there is a kind of slalom course. The players stand in two rows and first trot at an easy running pace along the inner side of the rows of balls. At the end of the course they turn, come easily back on the outside and can thus always practise in one round course. In addition to the simple warm-up exercises you can just as easily plan a large part of the fitness training on such a clearly laid out round course.

Warm-up

Exercise 1

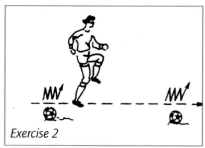

Exercise 2

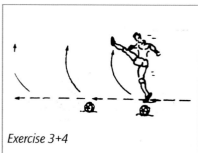

Exercise 3+4

Exercise 5

Exercise 6+7

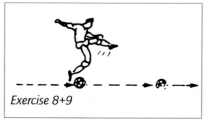

Exercise 8+9

Exercise 1: Easily Run and Hop. At each ball briefly hop on the spot.

Exercise 2: Stork Step - when walking exaggeratedly raise the thighs. A short raising of the knee at each ball.

Exercise 3: Walk, at each ball alternately swing your left and right leg forwards and backwards.

Exercise 4: Run, at each ball do a straddle, forward bends with bounce back (three times).

Exercise 5: Walk, alternately circle arms forwards and backwards.

Exercise 6: Run sideways, left and right, change at each ball.

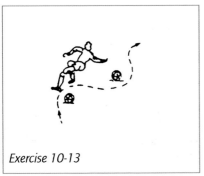

Exercise 10-13

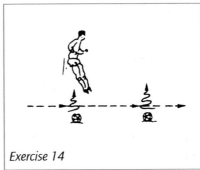

Exercise 14

Exercise 15-17

Exercise 18

Exercise 7: Run, at each ball crouch down, hands on the ground and bounce back (3 times).

Exercise 8: Adjusted steps, change at each ball.

Exercise 9: Run, at each ball a feigned kick (swing your leg out).

Exercise 10: Slalom run around the balls.

Exercise 11: Running backwards, slalom around balls.

Exercise 12: Running, at each ball a two-legged jump.

Exercise 13: The same, but with a header.

Exercise 14: Closing jumps over the balls.

Exercise 15: Running and intensifying jumps over the balls.

Exercise 16: Running and running around each ball.

Exercise 17: Accelerate, then easily run on, from ball to ball.

Exercise 18: Start backwards, at the ball turn briefly and quickly, accelerate to the next ball, turn and run backwards etc.

Exercise 19: Sprint to the ball, carry out a few powerful body feints before each ball, sprint to the next ball etc.

Main part

FIRST PART: INDEPENDENT ACCELERATION EXERCISES IN PAIRS
The players run easily across the playing field in pairs.

Exercise 1

Exercise 2

Exercise 3

Exercise 1: At a signal the second man starts off behind the first man with a fast acceleration (sprint over 10 m, then change places). 10 times (each player 5 times).

Exercise 2: The same exercise, but now the first man immediately dashes after his team-mate in order not to be shaken off - in spite of that person's body feints.

Exercise 3: The same exercise, but now the first man runs backwards and gets out of the way. When the second man starts his dash, the first man turns around and goes after him.

Exercise 4

Exercise 4: The same exercise, but now, with skilful movements, the running player backwards stops the other one getting past. He in turn tries to catch the first man on the wrong leg. After this exercise there is a short recovery break: relaxed passing.

SECOND PART: GROUP EXERCISES WITH THE BALL

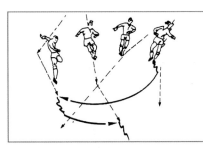

For this we need the whole field. We divide the players into 6 different groups: 2 groups with up to 6 players each and 4 groups with 2 to 4 players each. We divide the balls up in the following way: 4 or 5 balls in one goal, the same number at the centre line and one ball each at other positions (see sketch). The groups form up as shown in the picture. At a signal all the groups start. Group 1 starts with one ball from the goal line and - playing the ball back and forth - moves forward towards the centre line. On reaching it, the ball is deposited on the centre line and the players dash back to the starting point to get the next ball, etc. Group 2 does the same from the centre line to the other goal. Groups 3, 4, 5 and 6 get the ball from their particular starting position and combine until the next position. The ball stays there, the group sprints back etc.

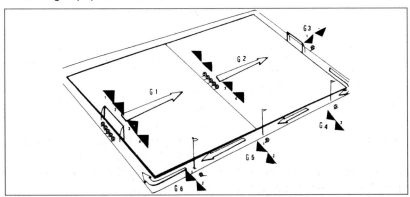

Combination exercises with players

Exercise 1: Each player is given a number and runs freely at a fairly high pace. At a signal 1 plays the ball to 2, he plays it on to 3 etc.. As soon as the ball reaches 1 again, have a short break and again combine, but now offer yourself with an acceleration. Increase the pace of execution and finally shorten the passes until you are working on a small part of the field at a high pace.

Exercise 2: Like Exercise 1, but now the player who was playing the ball takes the place of the player who receives the ball with a sprint (follow the ball).
Exercise 3: As a last variant combine completely freely, without a fixed order, with the emphasis on (free) running without the ball.

Training Session 28: Collective Change of Pace

In a previous training session we have carried out a number of exercises without the ball as an introduction to individual and collective changes of pace. Because towards the end of that training we were already well in momentum, we can now further develop these very important collective forms of behaviour which must become second nature. Good mastery of these automatisms is necessary in order to successfully fulfil the following tasks when in ball possession:
- Build up the game
- Use the element of surprise
- Achieve a certain degree of effectiveness
- Successfully start the counter-attack.
One thing is certain: Succeeding in the above stands and falls with the players passing at the right moment.

Warm-up

We want to start - in the warm-up already now - with what we finished in Training session 19: intersecting in various directions.
Formation: In a double row. We work across the width of the field and after every exercise the players swap places by running across in front of each other. We begin very calmly and easily, as appropriate to gradually warming up, increase the pace (also when changing places), so that at the end of the warm-up we have reached full speed.
Beginning: Easy skipping, at a signal cross over, again skipping etc. until the end of the field. While doing the warm-up exercises we have the opportunity to address all limbs and parts of the body: arms, legs, shoulders, torso, neck, joints etc. Begin slowly and systematically increase the pace. To give the players some variety get them to cross over running backwards a few times. To finish we get the players to cross over at full speed a few times. Go for good execution. Afterwards we repeat a pace and direction change a few times in alternation. Get the players to cross over at half-speed. At the whistle, each time a player starts at full speed - short dash - whereby the coach systematically reduces the time between the signals.

Main part

Exercise 1: We begin with an exercise which the players already know: Interception running of two players. Today we put the emphasis not only on crossing behind the opponent with the ball but also on sudden changes of pace without the ball. This exercise is mastered within a short time with short, powerful changes of pace and direction. Encourage the players and have them really exert themselves. In the well-earned break we divide the players into groups of three for the next exercise.

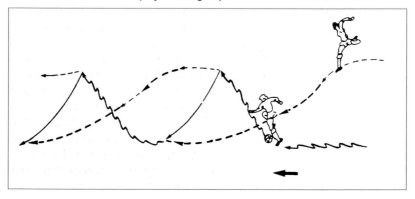

Exercise 2: With the addition of a third player we come to the next phase. At first the exercise is carried out exactly like the previous one: Interception running and playing the ball on. Now, however, the third player also crosses over behind the person with the ball each time - in the opposite direction to player 2. In the first series the person with the ball always plays towards team-mate 2 and only provides variety through diagonal sprints. In the second series the two back people without the ball alternate with accelerations in various directions, but always make sure that they can be played to at any time. The initiative lies with the person with the ball. He executes the pass when he thinks the time is right.

Exercise 3: We again add another player. Do not let the players develop too high a pace at the beginning of the exercise, make sure that each one changes pace and direction on time. After that we raise the pace, but continue to emphasise execution of the movements. In the second series we concentrate our attention on correct playing on of the ball. You can number the players from 1 to 4; they are then played to in order. It is better, however, to leave the initiative up to the players, starting with the person with the ball. The others move in such a way that they can always be played to. Afterwards the initiative comes from the players without the ball. Groups of 4 players thus move collectively across the field, with changing pace and constantly changing directions. A good start has been made and the players have fun. Set the duration of the exercise according to your estimation. It is not necessary to immediately carry out every training session described here. The aim of training is to teach the players something and that must not necessarily always be expressed in quantity.

Exercise 4: Attack with 6 players. Here the same principles apply as in the previous exercise. Begin slowly and end at a high pace. In the following we add a new aspect to the exercise. It is obvious that not all six players simply attack collectively. One player therefore remains in a waiting - securing - position. A second stays ready to support him. These need not always be the same players. The element of surprise lies in having these particular players move up. Their task is quickly taken over by a team-mate.

Exercise 3+4

Exercise 5+6

Exercise 7+8

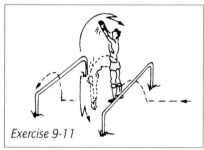

Exercise 9-11

Exercise 12

Exercise 3: Slalom around the hurdles and run back easily.

Exercise 4: Jump over the hurdles, stop, then crouch, bounce back up etc.

Exercise 5: Jump over the hurdles and between the hurdles circle arms, alternating forwards and backwards.

Exercise 6: Jump over the hurdles, always keeping arms outstretched at shoulder level.

Exercise 7: Run sideways and jump over the hurdles.

Exercise 8: Run a slalom around the hurdles backwards.

Exercise 9: Jump over hurdles, between the hurdles do forward bends with stretched legs, hands touch the ground, spring back once.

Exercise 10: Slalom around the hurdles at a fast pace.

Exercise 11: Acceleration, before the jump over the hurdles first execute a stretch jump, after landing going over the hurdle with a cushioning movement.

Exercise 12: Hop while crouching, then closing jump over the hurdle.

Exercise 13

Exercise 14

Exercise 15

Exercise 13: Alternately over and around the hurdle, jump over the first hurdle, then quickly run round the second, again over the third etc.

Exercise 14: Jump over the hurdles, while jumping do a header.

Exercise 15: Jump over the hurdle, while jumping half turn, then quickly turn around and accelerate to the next hurdle.

Main part

Note: Hurdles can be a good tool for carrying out exercises with high loads. Any of the exercises above can be used for this, you do not necessarily need 6 or 7 hurdles. One or two hurdles can be enough. An example: Set up in pairs. A flagpole is set up 5 metres from two hurdles. Player B gets into position 10 metres behind the hurdles, player A stands at the flagpole. At a signal (from B) A dashes over the hurdles to position 1, where he receives a pass from B, plays it back and immediately sprints back to the starting point (repeat 5 times, change). We can also use hurdle running very well for load intensive competitive games.

Some examples:
Three players at one end of the hurdle course and one player with a ball on the other side. At a signal player 1 starts and jumps over the hurdles. At the last jump player 2 throws the ball to player 1 who heads it back. At this moment player 3 starts. Meanwhile player 1 takes the place (and the ball) of player 2 who closes up at the other end of the hurdle course. Each player has 5 turns. Various groups can compete against each other.

Relay: All players at one end of the hurdle course (groups of three and four). Each player sprints down and comes back along the hurdles, releases the next man and lines up at the back.

Combination exercise: Players start (one second apart). On the way down jump over the hurdles and slalom back.

The difficulty here is not to mutually hinder each other, therefore the "jumpers" have the right of way. 5 times there and back, when the last man runs he is timed.

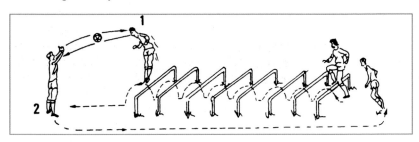

Training Session 30: Change of Pace in Practice

In training sessions 19 and 28 we covered some of the basic features of collective changes of pace and direction. With their introduction the question of course arises: How can we make use of this practically in the game? If we now practise the how and why in practical exercises we have already come quite a bit further. These exercises can be based on moves which often occur in games. Because these actions are repeated regularly, we develop automatisms: the players know what they have to do and what happens. Let us first take the wall pass. All elements occur in it and it can be used often. Today we want to use suitable exercises to come a little closer to our goal - developing automatisms.

Warm-up

This time we have a new formation variant: the star form - a simple formation which requires no preparation. Another advantage lies in the relaxed procedure: the players can talk to each other and the whole thing does not seem so organised as e.g. a prepared exercise course. It is, however, more difficult to check whether each player covers the prescribed course each time as the coach is in the centre of the star. The players execute the exercises on the way out each time and come back easily. While this is going on the coach gives them the next task so that when they reach the centre of the star they turn around without a break. We will carry out a number of "classic" exercises with or without the ball.

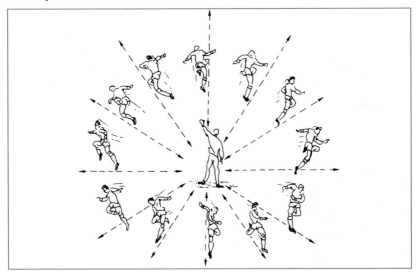

Main part

We have selected the following exercises for today:
- Attack in pairs
- Wall passes
- Attack in threes
- Build-up game in threes.

To start with we only carry out the movements from a technical aspect - without an opponent - until we have achieved a flowing sequence of motion. Afterwards we repeat the exercises under the aspect of unity of technique and tactics - with an opponent. Finally the players carry out the exercise completely freely but taking their assigned task into consideration.

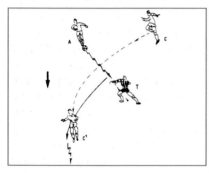

Exercise 1: Attack combination in pairs: Player A - in ball possession - stands opposite opponent T. He moves towards him with the ball while player C supports him with changes of pace and direction by sprinting past behind A's back.
Technical Emphasis: Change of pace by C and clean pass by A.
Tactical Emphasis: Keep the real intention secret as long as possible.

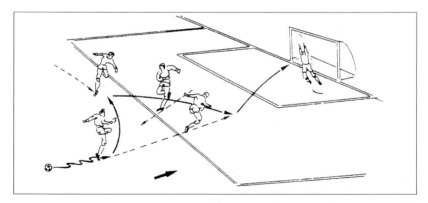

Exercise 2: Wall pass: One of the most frequently occurring combinations in the game, whereby two players together outplay an opponent. Individually outplaying by dribbling would also be possible, but using the wall pass is less risky. The wall pass can be used practically everywhere on the pitch: to break out of a defence

situation, to build up from the midfield and as a breakthrough on the attack. Today we will restrict ourselves to the wall pass in attacking, which is followed by a goal shot. It is, however, worthwhile devoting a whole training session to the wall pass with all its aspects. Wall pass practice: The player in possession of the ball must deal with an opponent. The attacker moves towards his opponent with the ball, but then plays to the left to his team-mate who plays the ball on past the opponent. (In training the free attacker - left - is a bouncing wall which is played to.) With a powerful acceleration run past the opposing player - receive the ball - shoot at goal.

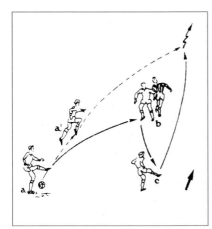

Exercise 3: Attack combination in threes. This action sequence is a means with which to be successful in the midfield - despite possible man coverage - or in the penalty area, to bring a forward or midfield player into the game. Player A (in ball possession) sees only one covered team-mate in front of him. Instead of going forwards with the ball at his foot himself - which would lead to a concentration of defenders - he plays to B and demonstratively acts as if his job is finished. Player B hides his real intentions as long as possible until he - covered behind - suddenly sends the ball back to C who plays to A further upfield as he suddenly dashes away.

Technical Emphasis:
- Clean pass from Player A to B
- Good coverage of the ball by B
- Direct passing on of the ball from B to C
- Accurate pass from C further upfield.

Tactical Emphasis:
- Rapid execution of the action sequence
- Proper training of C and also of A
- Hide the real intention as long as possible.

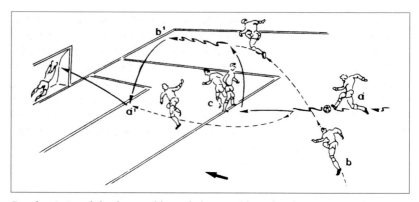

Exercise 4: Attack in threes with goal shot. In this action (a game situation which occurs frequently) we get closer to a bundling of changes of pace and direction. It is important that every player knows what his job is and which roles his team-mates have. This action is really a combination of the two previous moves and is a genuine game situation. Player A moves the ball towards team-mate B who, however, is covered behind. A plays to C while B suddenly takes off diagonally behind him into the depths of the field. As a diversion A calls to have the ball returned to him. Instead, C kicks the ball into the course of B. Player A waits briefly and pretends to maintain his position. Meanwhile B has run to the goal line and passes back to player A who expects this return play and dashes in explosively.

Exercise 5: Attack in threes. As with the previous exercises it is necessary to first execute the exercises technically cleanly in order to attain a flowing move. In addition to the accuracy of the pass, proper timing is absolutely necessary. Both

are necessary for a successful move. In this exercise we bring a midfield player across the centre into the attack. If this happens surprisingly, then an opportunity for a goal shot occurs. And that's what it's all about. Player A runs towards the opponent, then plays across to B who moves up in support. B shifts the game to the other side; this is the signal for A to suddenly break through with a forceful change of pace to then receive the ball back from B. Goal shot or move across to B or C (wall pass/one-two). After freely carrying out this exercise it is not over for the players. They remain constantly attentive and offer themselves. During free execution more defenders are involved.
This training ends with a short game.

Tactical Emphasis:
- Proper timing
- Rapid sequence of the individual phases
- Diversion and hide action as long as possible.
Technical Emphasis:
- Goal shot from rapid movement.

Training Session 31: Fitness Training with Medicine Balls

Exercises with medicine balls are an indispensable element of fitness training. Running exercises dominate, i.e. the leg muscles. Although as soccer players we must of course train these muscles well, a change of load to also use the other muscles is more than welcome. And here the use of the medicine ball is appropriate. It allows strength exercises which can be carried out with gusto.

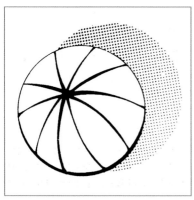

Warm-up

Line up in two rows across the width of the field. The players in the right row have one ball each. At the edge of the field the ball is handed over to the partner who works with the ball on the way back.

Exercise 1

Exercise 2

Exercise 3

Exercise 4

Exercise 1: While walking throw the ball up and catch it (with cushioning movement).

Exercise 2: While skipping alternately hold the ball above your head with both hands outstretched or in front of your chest.

Exercise 3: Run easily and throw the ball back and forth (turn your torso well in doing so).

Exercise 4: While hopping on one leg roll the ball forwards with your foot (sole), every 10 steps change feet.

Exercise 5:
As in Exercise 3, but now one of the players runs backwards.

Exercise 6:
Run. At a signal, put the ball down between your legs 10 times per run, jump up twice, closing your feet above the ball, run on.

Exercise 7:
Run sideways and throw the ball to your partner.

Exercise 8:
As in Exercise 6, but now jump forwards and backwards over the ball.

Main part

Exercise 1

Exercise 2

Exercise 3

Exercise 4

Exercise 5

Exercise 1: Players A and B stand back-to-back in a straddle: hand over the ball - in the form of an eight; a circle.

Exercise 2: Players A and B stand 3 to 5 m apart. Throw the ball to each other and catch it with a cushioning movement. Variant: Throw the ball low across the ground.

Exercise 3: As in Exercise 2, but player A throws the ball high, player B catches it and throws it back low. Increase speed and distance.

Exercise 4: Player A throws the ball as in a throw-in. Player B catches it jumping. Variant: A throws jumping.

Exercise 5: The player throws the ball to the partner who catches it with his foot.

EXERCISES IN FOURS

Some game forms two against two:

Exercise 1: Pass the ball throwing.

Exercise 2: Play the ball to the partner.

Exercise 3: The ball is rolled.

Exercise 4: The ball is picked up off the ground, thrown and after being caught immediately placed on the ground again.

GAME

All of these options can be used for a game with the medicine ball (very strenuous).

Training Session 32: Team Talk

In spite of all good resolutions and efforts it is possible that success in the points game eludes us. Success is dependent on many factors and chance also plays a role. The coach prepares himself as well as possible, he uses all his ability. But in the eyes of many his qualities are still determined by a shot above or below the crossbar. Without wanting to speak of a crisis meeting, at today's training there will be a discussion with the players of the first team - the core - while the other players train normally. The conversation could be like this:

Why have we come together for this talk?
• The team does not have a specific spearhead. We therefore need to find solutions which lie in the support of the midfield.
• Because of a major injury of the sweeper (out of action for the rest of the season), we need to find a replacement although nobody is especially suited for this position.
Physically the players are fit. They try to play as is required of them, but they are not playing with an element of surprise. The lack of attacking players can only be compensated by active help from the midfield and that does not always occur as

it should. Because of the sudden changed situation (injury) a solution must also be found for the defence. There, new moves must be practised and automatised which the players can fully accept.

Stocktaking of progress to date

Club management: Everyone has made an effort to put together as talented a player core as possible. They thus have high expectations.

Coach: He knows he has players available to him who can prove their merit in this championship. He came to this club particularly because of the great commitment which this team was always able to bring. Injuries cannot be predicted, but if they do occur we cannot restrict ourselves to complaining.

The coach to the players: You don't need to worry, we just want to take an objective look at where we are and what we need to do. As players we need to finish the season together. Nobody is seen as a scapegoat. We have to master this situation as a team. The wishes of the coach remain only wishes, but the team spirit of the team brings the successes. On Sunday we have to get on the pitch again, week after week, and then only results count, not moaning or excuses. I assumed responsibility for the team because I believe in you. And I still believe in you just as firmly. We just have to openly consider our condition and not be scared to talk about it. We don't play badly. It is just a small thing which keeps tripping us up. But to be honest, our game is not that great either. Simply because this so-called small thing keeps occurring every week. I have analysed the first games. We know our strengths. We are a community of friends and every one of you can play good soccer. If we look at our excellent initial results then we know that we can master the situation. How have we done so far? We win two games, play undecided once and keep losing 1:0. No great games, but the commitment was always there. Now we could excuse the extremely close defeats and point to the injury of the sweeper, but the real reason must be sought elsewhere. For apart from commitment a few other things are necessary:

- Concentration and following instructions
- Receiving the ball and getting it under control quickly
- Allocating energy and playing the ball in time (better in the first game and now, why?)
- Running without the ball on the attack (must be done even if it "hurts")
- Taking the last decisive pass (only possible if the previous points have been realised), otherwise we give away the element of surprise.
- Not playing ponderously and lethargically but making sure there are surprises and explosions (change of pace).
- Every player must have a proper understanding of his job (of himself and of the team).

Discussion

Note: After a hesitant start, thanks to the coach's positive questions the players really got going and spoke frankly. Afterwards we sorted the comments and formulated a number of conclusions.

• Support the attack more effectively from the midfield.
• When the ball is lost everyone must energetically cover their man.
• Do not lose too much time in the midfield through petty play. This could be achieved by moving up forwards from the midfield so that more possibilities to be played to are created.
• Run freely without the ball more often.
• "Peter" (midfield player): Defend and get organised more in the mid-field. When in ball possession he is the build-up player and the man who can be played to in any difficult situation. But he himself should not go along as much. He helps and is the switching station between defence and midfield. When the ball is lost he is the buffer in front of the defence (delay).
• "Herman" (midfield player): Should orientate himself more to the attack, would like to play behind the forwards because he likes defending less. Just like the forwards he must disrupt when the ball is lost.
• Forwards: Because there are two of them they have to work a lot and move around and create chances for others.
• Defence players: Take on the defence role even more.

The defence task has priority; as far as possible they support the attack during a build-up (one of them happens to have an attitude of being on the offensive). When there are corner kicks one of our "two big boys" comes out of the defence and moves up front.

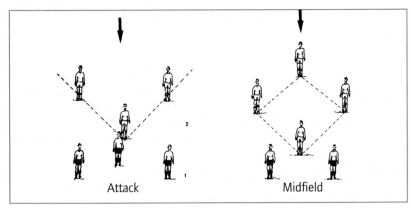

Attack   Midfield

The diagram shows the systems which finally resulted. With the defence moved up. Move back when the ball is lost and strengthen the midfield.
The training was continued with:
1. Cooper Test (12 minute test)
2. Pushed fitness training in which the players especially exert themselves (they were noticeably motivated). Some of the exercises are shown below.

Warm-up

In particular address the legs, torso and shoulders. Duration: 10 minutes.

Main part

PUSHED INTERVAL TRAINING

Because the pitch is being used by players who are not part of the core, we train next to it. The fact that the core players are "seen" will stimulate the others additionally. Load is applied in series of 5 in all cases. After each series there is a short break. 20 minutes of load are followed by a quarter of an hour of recovery.

Exercise 1

Exercise 2

Exercise 3

Exercise 4

Exercise 5

Exercise 1: Hard acceleration to 50 % of maximum speed.
Exercise 2: Hard acceleration to maximum speed, with a change of pace.
Exercise 3: Accelerate hard. At half the distance lower the pace and accelerate again.

Exercise 4: In pairs. Always try to keep next to each other.
Exercise 5: In pairs. The first player accelerates, the second closes up and after reducing speed then dashes off himself etc.

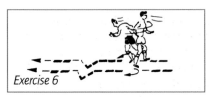

Exercise 6

Exercise 7

Exercise 8

Exercise 6: Run backwards, turn round and accelerate (in pairs).

Exercise 7: In pairs. A runs backwards, B forwards, A accelerates, tries to block, then turns round and pursues A.

Exercise 8: Try to shake off a partner with all sorts of movements.

Exercise 9: Series of short dashes over 5 m in fast sequence.
a) Forwards
b) Under load each time diagonally sideways to the left or right
c) First stop, then accelerate
d) First 2 m back, then accelerate forwards.

14 Training Playing for Points (High Season)

Training Session 33: Goalkeeper Training

Really we should develop a separate annual programme for this topic. Regrettably goal keeper training is often neglected. Frequently this training consists of a few shots at the goal, and that in such a way which makes little or no sense from the point of view of an effective goal keeper training. Despite this everyone knows that the goalkeeper is one of the cornerstones - if not the most important - in the team. Because his responsibilities differ greatly from those of the outfield players it goes without saying that the training and coaching of the goalkeeper must logically recognise this. After all, in modern soccer the role of the goalkeeper is not limited to catching a few balls, he must also be familiar with the role of the outfield players, at least with regard to the playing system and the automatisms. In practice it is not easy for a coach to occupy himself intensively with the outfield players, and in addition also with the goalkeeper. On the other hand, not every coach is assisted by a goalkeeper coach. With a little goodwill and some planning, however, this can be solved. By the way, it is important that the goalkeeper is involved in the whole game as much as possible in addition to this, if only because it is necessary for his physical condition and his contact to the team. A complete training course for goalkeepers cannot be covered here. We will a limit ourselves to season training. If we summarise the most important characteristics and qualities as well as the typical responsibilities of a goalkeeper we already have a good basis on which we can build up a programme. Observation of the game situations teaches us that the tasks of the goalkeeper require the following:

- Skills with the ball: catching, punching, diverting, keeping the ball under control, hitting away, throwing away;
- Skills without the ball: positional play, running out, covering the goal, jumping.

The goalkeeper defends not only his goal but in addition intercepts attacks and introduces the attack of his own 11. The following is also expected of a goalkeeper: good reaction ability, mobility, suppleness and strength. Assuming these prerequisites, we can develop a programme and know how sound training must be structured. With goalkeeper training too we ask the questions already mentioned, again in the interest of preparation:

- Which exercises do we carry out?
- Why do we carry out these exercises (Objective)?
- How will we teach these exercises (Execution)?

In doing so we also note that goalkeeper training also consists of three parts:

- Warm-up
- Main part
- Warm-down

Warm-up

As a warm-up at each training we carry out:
- Easy running and jumping exercises
- Exercises for the legs
- Exercises for the arms
- Torso exercises
- Sprints.

The main part should include:
- General strengthening exercises: legs, arms, shoulders, stomach, back and adductors
- Development of condition and jumping power
- Development of reaction ability and overview
- Goalkeeping technique
- Game-technical training
- Game-tactical training

With goalkeeper training we have the advantage we can work with a very small group. Contact is close, you can talk to each other during the exercises and it is fairly easy to organise. In order to create as many basic prerequisites as possible it seems to us to make sense to give a number of the example exercises for each of the points described, so that with their help you can develop your own training.

Warm-up programme

Warm-up can be done individually or in pairs (in groups), with and without the ball.

Exercise 1:
Run easily and loosen up all muscles

Exercise 2:
Skip, shake out the muscles.

Exercise 3:
Calm knee raising run.

Exercise 4:
Walk while turning your torso, looking at the hand of the half outstretched arm.

Exercise 5

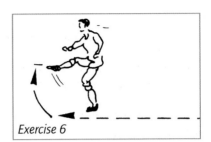

Exercise 6

Exercise 7

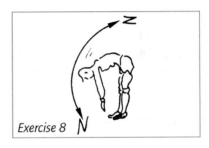

Exercise 8

Exercise 9

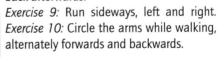

Exercise 10

Exercise 5: One-legged jumps, alternating left and right, after every 5 steps, change over.

Exercise 6: Walk, at every third step raise the stretched leg to hip level.

Exercise 7: Circle your head right and left, tilting your head forwards and backwards.

Exercise 8: Forward bends with springing back afterwards.

Exercise 9: Run sideways, left and right.

Exercise 10: Circle the arms while walking, alternately forwards and backwards.

It is recommendable to begin with simple exercises so that the players do not have to think of anything and can really run until they are loosened up. Between the exercises also trot around easily. Greatly increase the pace of these "loosening runs".

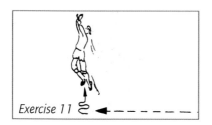

Exercise 11

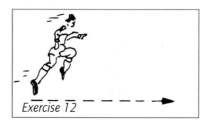

Exercise 12

Exercise 11: Run, at a signal jump (25 times). Systematically increase jumping height.
Exercise 12: To finish, accelerate hard and sprint a few times.

Some examples for an individual warm-up with the ball: We begin very easily again. To begin with the ball is not yet the objective, but rather a tool to support the movements. Simply circling the body with the ball already activates a large number of the muscles.

Exercise 1

Exercise 2

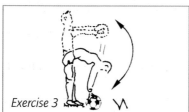

Exercise 3

Exercise 4

Exercise 5

Exercise 1: Run easily, throw the ball up and catch it (very elastically).

Exercise 2: While running bounce the ball on the ground and catch the ball as it springs up.

Exercise 3: Walk, hold the ball out in front of you with stretched arms: forward bend, bring the ball to the ground and spring back.

Exercise 4: Run easily and bounce the ball left and right.

Exercise 5: Hold the ball in both hands, arms outstretched. Swing your arms from left to right and back or diagonally upwards and back.

Exercise 6

Exercise 7

Exercise 8

Exercise 9

Exercise 10

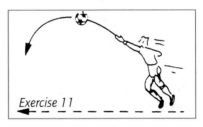

Exercise 11

Exercise 6: Run easily, holding the ball in both hands. While running jump and hold the ball as high as possible.

Exercise 7: While walking circle the ball around your body and follow it with your eyes as long as possible.

Exercise 8: At every third step swing your outstretched leg up high, left and right, pass the ball quickly under your leg.

Exercise 9: Drop the ball, pull it back up with your foot and catch it.

Exercise 10: While running throw the ball up high and while jumping up catch it. Try to systematically increase your jumping height.

Exercise 11: While running throw the ball forwards diagonally and dash up to catch it.

Loosen up between the various exercises, but always with the ball: throw, catch, circle it around your body, throw, catch and hold it in front of your chest etc. The ball is your partner, not your opponent.

STRETCHING EXERCISES WITHOUT THE BALL

Carry out the stretching exercises at a pace which is not too high - with springing back or stretching. We also make sure that as great an amplitude of movement as possible is achieved. The emphasis is on careful execution and the repeats.

Legs and Arms

Exercise 1

Exercise 2

Exercise 3

Exercise 4

Exercise 5

Exercise 6

Exercise 1: Alternately swing left and right leg forwards, upwards and back.

Exercise 2: Forward bends, hands touch the ground, straighten up, hold arms up high.

Exercise 3: Crouch, hands on hips (or on the ground), alternately stretch your left leg and right leg to the side and spring back.

Exercise 4: Arms held up high, in a continuous movement forward bends and swing your arms down and behind through your straddled legs and spring back.

Exercise 5: Alternately swing your left and right leg easily forwards and upwards.

Exercise 6: Crouch, hands on the ground - frog jump up hight. Support the upwards movement by swinging your arms up.

Exercise 7

Exercise 8

Exercise 9

Exercise 7: Swing your arms high as far as your body can reach, swing back down and spring back.

Exercise 8: Alternately swing arms forwards and backwards.

Exercise 9: Swing your arms to the side and down.

Stomach muscle exercises

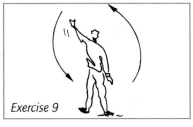

Exercise 1

Exercise 2

Exercise 3

Exercise 1: Lie on your back, arms and legs stretched away from you: raise your legs still stretched and lower them again slowly. Variant: with your feet touch the ground behind your head.

Exercise 2: Sidewards straddle, arms held up high: bend your upper body backwards as far as you can and slowly return to the starting position.

Exercise 3: Lie on your back, arms stretched, raise your stretched legs to a vertical position and cycle.

Back muscle exercises

After the stomach muscle exercises it is recommendable to carry out a few exercises for the back muscles as compensation.

Exercise 1

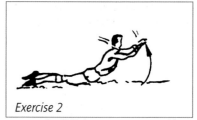

Exercise 2

Exercise 1: Lie on your stomach, arms and legs stretched. Raise your arms and legs as far as possible, then slowly move back.

Exercise 2: Lie on your stomach arms and legs stretched. Raise your arms and torso as far as possible. Legs stay on the ground. Slowly move back.

Exercises for the torso

Exercise 1

Exercise 2

Exercise 3

Exercise 1: Straddle, arms held at the side: Alternately turn to the left and right and spring back with outstretched arms (twice)

Exercise 2: Sideways straddle, torso bent forward: touch your left foot with your right hand, stretch the other arm upwards and backwards; then the left hand to the right foot, right hand to left foot etc.

Exercise 3: Sideways straddle, hands on hips: alternately forward bends, sideways to the left and right, spring back.

STRETCHING EXERCISES WITH THE BALL

Now we can immediately carry out a number of exercises using the ball. The ball is still not the objective, but the tool. It is an advantage that the goalkeeper can use the object (ball) he must deal with in this form already and thus become more familiar with it. Some examples:

Legs

Exercise 1

Exercise 2

Exercise 3

Exercise 1: Walk, every three steps raise a leg up high and pass the ball under the leg.

Exercise 2: Partial sideways straddle, hold the ball up high: forward bend and with the ball touch the ground to the left and right in front of your feet.

Exercise 3: Hold the ball in front of your body at shoulder level. While walking, touch the ball with your knee at every third step.

Arms

Exercise 1:
While walking throw the ball up high and catch it with both hands.

Exercise 2
While walking stretch ball up high, or drop it, let it bounce and catch it again.

Torso

Exercise 1

Exercise 2

Exercise 3

Exercise 1: Sideways straddle: circle the ball with outstretched arms to the left and right of your body.
Exercise 2: While walking swing the ball behind you with your hands (turn torso) and follow it with your eyes.
Exercise 3: Circle your body with the ball, as far as possible move out of the way with your hips.

Exercises in pairs

Because in practice during training we normally do not only work with the goalkeeper, the exercises can be organised in such a way that both players work together. Some examples:

Exercise 1

Exercise 1: Throw the ball backwards and forwards
- at knee level
- from below to chest level
- at jumping height
- in front of your partner (too short)

Exercise 2

Exercise 4

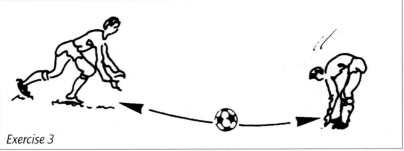

Exercise 3

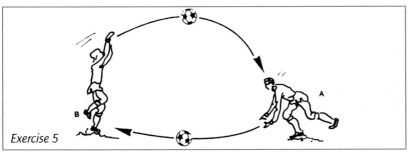

Exercise 5

Exercise 2: Crouch, hold hands: Cossack dance.

Exercise 3: Roll the ball to each other, taking up with stretched legs
- to the man
- to the left and right next to your partner.

Exercise 4: Partial sideways straddle, back-to-back at a distance of 1 m: pass the ball on turning quickly:
- in the form of a figure 8
- in a circle.

Exercise 5: Player A throws the ball at knee level, B catches it and throws it back high.

Exercise 6

Exercise 7

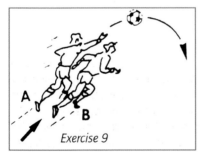

Exercise 8

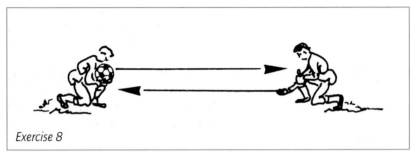

Exercise 9

Exercise 10

Exercise 6: Side straddle, back to back 1 m apart: pass the ball through your legs and over your heads.

Exercise 7: Player A runs backwards, player B forwards. Throw the ball to each other: - high - hard at chest level - as a bouncing ball.

Exercise 8: Both players kneel with one leg, left or right. Throw the ball backwards and forwards hard and low: - at the partner - to the left and right next to the partner (systematically increase the distance) - above head level.

Exercise 9: The players run next to each other. Player A throws the ball high, B accelerates and catches the ball while A runs behind and disrupts (passively).

Exercise 10: The players sit back to back and pass each other the ball at the side.

Exercise 11

Exercise 12

Exercise 13

Exercise 11: The players run 7 to 8 m apart. A throws the ball straight up, B dashes to A's place to catch the ball. A takes B's place.

Exercise 12: Kneel on one leg: throw the ball up high and jump up to catch it.

Exercise 13: Throw the ball to each other hard and fast at chest level.

STRENGTH EXERCISES

The exercises are certainly necessary for a goalkeeper. In order to be master of his penalty area goalkeeper must not only have technique and playing intelligence but also sufficient strength. He must always master the situation in direct confrontation with one or more opponents and keep the opponent away from the ball. Here we show a number of exemplary strength exercises which are suitable for goal keeper training. They complement the normal strength exercises carried out during training with the core team.

Exercise 1

Exercise 1: Piggyback under the aspect of fitness: Carry another person over a longer distance, at a higher pace or: short but with many fast changeovers.

Exercise 2

Exercise 3

Exercise 4

Exercise 5

Exercise 2: Wheelbarrow. Begin slowly. Gradually increase the pace and distance. Or: short distances, but fast changes.

Exercise 3: Carry your partner vertically or horizontally before your chest for a long distance.

Exercise 4: Leapfrog. Emphasis on take-off (height) or emphasis on pace (jumping frequency).

Exercise 5: Rocking back to back, arms linked: take turns at bending forward. Emphasise bending low or fast execution (higher frequency). The medicine ball can also be used regularly for strength exercises. The exercises are somewhat more demanding of jumping strength and are more game-like, but very strenuous.

Exercise 6: Partial side straddle, hold the ball in front of you and lift it over your head. Variant: Hold the ball up - crouch - put the ball on the ground and back.

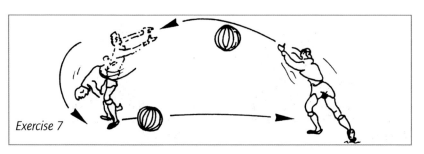

Exercise 7

Exercise 8

Exercise 49

Exercise 10

Exercise 11

Exercise 7: Player A (with his back to B) throws the ball through his legs towards B. The latter catches the ball and throws it back high. A catches the ball, turning his torso in doing so. Do not change the position of your feet.

Exercise 8: Throw the ball back and forth. Thrusting throw from the chest. Catch it with both hands before your chest and throw it back immediately.

Exercise 9: Throw-in. Jump up to catch the ball and throw it back immediately. After 10 throws change places.

Exercise 10: Throw backwards and forwards while running.

Exercise 11: Closing jumps over the ball. Or: side straddle over the ball, jumps up and land in a straddle again.

Fitness training

We must spend a major part of the season working on the goalkeeper's fitness. For the goalkeeper must always be top fit and in unpredictable situations also defend his goal successfully, mostly under great pressure and against relentless opponents who seek their chance one after the other with all their might. In addition to the regular training for the core team - in which the goalkeeper naturally participates - it is a good idea to work out a specific goalkeeper training taking the requirements of a goalkeeper into consideration: Running, jumping, diving, sudden braking of a movement in order to switch to another movement. In doing this we use a ball. Here we are not yet speaking of training technique, but of a fitness build-up in which, however, both the amount of load and also speed have priority. In order to have a rapid sequence of exercises we make sure there are enough balls available. A ball boy helps to get the ball back.

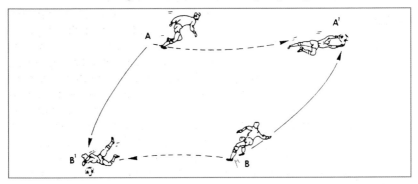

Exercise 1: The two goalkeepers stand opposite each other in a square 15 m x 15m. At a signal player B throws the ball to position A1 and dashes to the left. A dashes to the right and dives after the thrown ball. Both players begin easily and systematically raise the pace and the hardness of the throws. This exercise is also useful later as a "pressure training", but then at full speed.

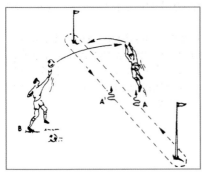

Exercise 2: Run between two flagpoles: Player A starts at on flagpole, receives the pass (throw) from Player B and immediately throws back. If the accent is on speed, player A increases his running speed while B constantly throws the ball at chest level. If the emphasis is on ball control, player B increases the degree of difficulty with his passes. The best thing is to do both at the same time. Also ideal for a "tempo training": e.g. run 5 full rounds and change over.

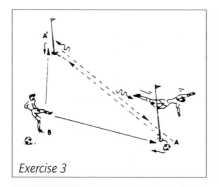

Exercise 3

Exercise 4

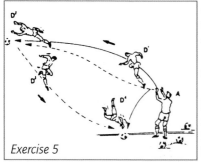

Exercise 5

Exercise 3: A game-like variant: Player A runs as in the previous exercise, but catches the ball behind the flagpoles. Here too the accents can be set differently. If speed is to be emphasised, B throws in such a way that A gets the ball when changing direction and throws it back. If the accent is on catching the ball, the passes force the player to throw himself to the ball and then afterwards to run more easily back to the other side. If you combine both, you have a very difficult exercise (execute quickly). Spur the players on so that they give their all.

Exercise 4: For the following exercise we only need one flagpole: The goalkeeper sprints away from the flagpole. At a call his partner places the ball directly behind him. The goalkeeper stops and throws himself at the ball. Variant 1: The partner no longer calls out where he will place the ball, but throws it to roughly the same place. Variant 2: The partner now places the ball wherever he wants - with and without a call. Regularly swap roles.

Exercise 5: Here two tasks follow each other. First A throws the ball away a few metres (high and far), goalkeeper B sprints in, gets the ball under control (jumping or diving) and throws it back to A. Meanwhile A plays the ball short, which must be brought under control by the goalkeeper as quickly as possible (5 times, then change). Emphasis on pace, with the second ball again give everything.

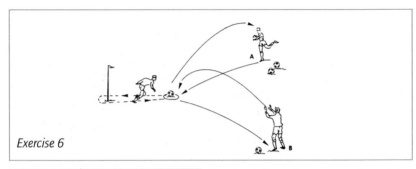

Exercise 6

Exercise 7

Exercise 8

Exercise 6: Two players pass alternately - player A low and player B high. The goalkeeper dashes from the flagpole (5 m away) and throws himself on the ball. He throws each ball back accurately (throw out), over shorter distances from below, over longer distances from above, Alternately low over the ground and high. We can increase the distance or the pace

Exercise 7: We use a hurdle or several hurdles in order to do justice to a new aspect - namely jumping. The goalkeeper runs, with the ball in both hands, towards the hurdle, throws the ball under the hurdle, jumps over the hurdle himself and throws himself after the ball. Variant: Now he throws the ball high while jumping and catches it before it touches the ground.

Exercise 8: Jumps from a standstill, whereby the goalkeeper must fight for the ball against a passive opponent. The goalkeeper stands behind his opponent and jumps after the ball up which is thrown over the head of his opponent, and throws the ball back from below. We can increase the throwing height and the throw-in frequency. In order to increase the degree of difficulty, in later rounds we can place the ball next to the opposing player. Hereby the emphasis remains on jumping strength and not on technical aspects of catching the ball.

Exercise 9

Exercise 10

Exercise 9: Jump after an additional task: The goalkeeper must first run around one or two opposing players before he throws himself on the ball which has been thrown (jump or dive). Turn very shortly and quickly, get the take-off right.

Exercise 10: The goalkeeper crawls between the legs of a player and then throws himself on the ball which has been thrown (jump or dive).

Technical exercises

Goalkeeper training is very intensive for both those involved because the coach actively participates in the exercises. Therefore good organisation is important. We must already know beforehand which exercises we want to use and how these should be executed. Enough material, someone who gathers up the balls, choosing the right distance and player and recovery breaks save much energy. On the other hand, it is a pleasant way of training because one is actively involved oneself and stands in close contact to the players. This allows the coach to discover strengths and weaknesses in the technical and the human areas.

When doing technique training we pay attention to exact and correct execution (position of the hands and the body as well as posture) and to the sequence of movements. At the same time we constantly give the necessary corrections. Encouragement and comments about executions that are not so good should be given. Comments about good execution after correction should not be exaggerated, however. It is best if we start a few metres away from the goalkeeper; the ball is thrown. The advantage is that the rate is higher and the throws always arrive accurately so that the goalkeeper can receive the ball in a technically sensible way. Always practise from three throwing directions: in front of the player, to the left and right of the player. Hands (how was the ball received), body and the legs (shield the ball) all play a major role in all exercises.

1 *Exercise 1* 2

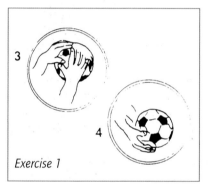

Exercise 1

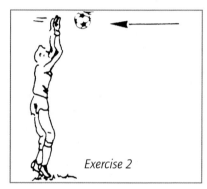

Exercise 2

Exercise 1: Catching the ball at chest level (1 and 2). We throw the ball from a few metres away. At the beginning not too hard, gradually increase hardness and distance. Finally play the ball with your foot. High balls are held with the hands (3), then the ball is drawn to the chest, whereby the goalkeeper bends over the ball. Distance shots are caught (4) and also clasped to the chest. With harder balls the chest serves as a "shock absorber" in order to break up the force of flying balls. Therefore the body must always be well behind the ball. A frequent mistake: The ball is not caught softly enough and therefore jumps away; bad positioning of the hands (only half behind the ball), as a result of which the ball is not stopped; the body is not properly behind the ball, and the chest has not followed properly, therefore the ball does not stay under control.

Exercise 2: Catching high balls without jumping. Here both phases of the previous exercises are combined. The ball is stopped (not held onto) (3), comes down and is brought under control in front of the chest close (4). Both phases cannot be separated from each other, they flow into each other. Practice well with hard shots. Most common mistake: The hands are not brought up behind the ball properly. One tends to want to "pluck" the ball, so that it slips through. At this moment (the ball is still above the head) you have no other defence option than your hands!

Exercise 3

Exercise 4

Exercise 3: Catching balls when jumping from a standing position. Here the same rules apply as in the previous exercises plus timing and execution of the jump. Execute the jump in such a way that the ball is stopped at its highest point. Raise one knee for protection (applies to all jumps). Most common mistake: Wrong timing and not enough jumping power.

Exercise 4: Catching rolling or very low balls. These balls can be caught in two ways: With outstretched legs or with one knee on the ground. Which one you decide on depends on your mobility. It is obvious that when standing you have more freedom to move, but on the other hand you have to be more agile to catch the ball safely. Half kneeling, on the other hand, provides more security for catching itself. The supporting foot points obliquely in the direction of the ball, whereby the knee of the other leg is held closely to the supporting foot or just above the ground in order to provide protection behind the hands. Most common mistake: The foot is held straight in front of the body so that the knees hinder arm movements; too great a distance between supporting foot and knee of the other leg; wrong timing when catching the ball - this then jumps away. Watch out for bouncing balls.

Exercise 5   *Exercise 6*

Exercise 5: Diving after a "long" ball. For the spectators, diving after a very long ball is certainly one of the most spectacular moments in a game. For the goalkeeper it is important to apply the right technique, which is very different for low and high balls. One certainly regularly sees very beautiful dives after low balls where, however, the goalkeeper comes a fraction of a second too late. Very beautiful leaps perfect for publication in a newspaper, but which really were not necessary; a cleaner jump which was not so high would have been more appropriate. The low dive can best be learned from the crouch. Balls are placed further and further away from the goalkeeper. Practise the technique of a side-step, the take off and falling to the side. Grasping the ball (one hand behind and one on the ball) and drawing it to your chest are easier afterwards. Most common mistake: Not throwing oneself after the ball, rather falling on the ball; one hand is not behind the ball; the ball is not drawn to the chest and shielded with the body.

Exercise 6: Catching high balls with a dive. This is one of the most difficult techniques which generally determines the quality of a goalkeeper. The flight towards the ball and the necessary techniques should really be learnt from early youth on because then you have time to learn the various elements of this technique in the sand pit. With a side-step the goalkeeper moves to the side where a ball is expected in order to properly place his jumping leg. He takes off on the "inner" leg, i.e. the leg closest to the jumping direction, and shifts his weight on to this leg for this purpose. In the air he brings his hands behind the ball (3). Now comes the most difficult part: landing with the ball in your hands. Do not fall flat on your stomach, but drop to the ground with your whole body in one movement. Cushion the first shock with your hands, gather up the ball, then your body rolls on over your arms, shoulders and hips. Don't forget to shield the ball with your body. Falling has to be learnt, just think of Judo experts; this is a technique of its own which you cannot learn early enough. Most common mistake: Incorrect landing and letting go of the ball; bad clasping of the ball. Watch out for the goal posts!

Exercise 7

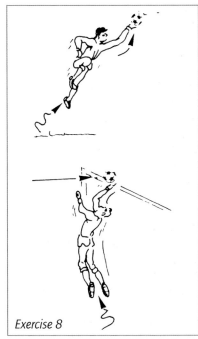

Exercise 8

Exercise 7: Punching in the air. A way of preventing a goal which is not so safe is simply diverting the ball by punching it away. It is not so safe because doing this you do not get the ball under control and it is also more difficult to repulse the ball because of the smaller hitting area. Sometimes, however, the goalkeeper is forced to use this technique: When the ball gets between number of players jumping in the air; when the ball is simply too far away to catch, etc. As far as possible, use both fists so that the hitting area is greater. In addition it is necessary to always include the follow-through after punching (namely immediately be present again), because there is a great likelihood that the ball remains in play. Most common mistake: Punching away wins the upper hand (disadvantages mentioned); incorrect timing on take-off which is of great significance because you only have a fraction of a second to bring fist and ball in contact with each other; the ball is not punched far enough away, or the jump to the ball is not concluded (goal is left under very dangerous conditions).

Exercise 8: Diverting the ball with your fingers. This is also a technique which we use in emergencies when the ball is too far away to catch or punch it. Preferably, use your palm and bend your elbows, which turns the ball outwards - slightly give way with your hand.

In the case of very hard centres and certainly also corner kicks a ball which is too high can often be diverted over the goal with your fingers. Consider, though, that diverting with one hand allows a greater range than diverting with both hands. Most common mistake: Goalkeeper does not hold his wrist firmly enough so that his hand is hit away from the ball.

We can really put other ways of hitting the ball away under the term "outfield play". Kicking away the ball, stopping it with the chest, intercepting a ball with your thigh or your foot and heading away the ball will certainly become part of the goalkeepers repertoire if he is included in normal training and games enough, in which one can use him as a "normal" outfield player without hesitation.

But the goalkeeper not only has a defending function. He is also involved in offensive play. At least always when he's in possession of the ball he should play the first pass to build up the attack. By involving the goalkeeper - passing to the goalkeeper - the game can be shifted to the other side in a safe way. Here the goalkeeper has two different techniques: kicking away and throwing away (rolling) the ball. When kicking the goalkeeper will usually use the drop kick. With regard to throwing he can either throw from below or above.

Exercise 1

Exercise 2

Exercise 1: Kicking away of a standing ball. The goalkeeper regulates his run-up in such a way that the last step ends next to the ball, i.e. the standing leg is also next to the ball. The instep of his kicking leg is pushed down and hits the ball completely; follow through with your leg afterwards.

Exercise 2: Kicking away the ball from your hands (drop-kick). Once he has the ball the goalkeeper will kick it away as far as possible. As shown in the diagram, he takes a run-up. Variant 1 (no drop-kick): Kick the ball in the air (with a powerful kick both legs are off the ground). Variant 2: Kick the ball at the moment this bounces up from the ground. Pay attention to your standing leg which is placed next to the ball.

Exercise 3

Exercise 4

Exercise 5

Exercise 3: Throw-out. In order to put the ball back into play over a short distance the throw is an appropriate method. Do not just throw the ball back (bounce, feints etc), but choose the proper technique. Safety is most important.

Rolling: Roll the ball with a flowing movement over the ground to your partner. Such a pass is easy for your team mate to receive.

Exercise 4: Shock throw. In the case of greater distances the goalkeeper can throw from below. In this way the trajectory of the ball remains relatively low and the ball is easy to receive.

Exercise 5: Throw-out from below. With a little practice the goalkeeper can get the ball to the player chosen by him over a fairly great distance and with greater certainty than with a kick away. Most common mistakes:

Kick away: - Standing leg placed wrongly - Foot not stretched out - The ball is not hit properly (back position) - the ball is only touched

Drop-kick: - Foot is to far under the ball (high and not far) - Weak foot movement, more a movement from the knees

Throw-out: - The ball is let go of too late, in the case of throwing out from below (shock throw) the ball then goes up (lob), and by throwing out from above (punch throw) it is bounced on the ground. - The hand is not consistently behind the ball, instead the ball is just grazed, gets an enormous side spin and is thus hard to receive because it does not go in the desired direction. In modern soccer the fast and precise throw-out of the ball has become an important element of the fast game. Therefore the goalkeeper must be sufficiently trained for this task.

Independent training

Here is an example for training at home which the goalkeeper can do daily.

Independent Training

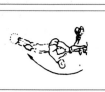
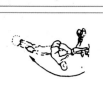

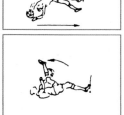
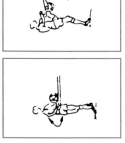

Exercise	Execution	Series
Turning the Torso. Partial Straddle. The ball is behind the goalkeeper at hip level (e.g. on a table. Turn, take the ball, turn around, put the ball down etc.	Two series of 10, after the first series 10 seconds break	Later: 2 x 15 and 2 x 20
Swing the leg up high in front. Ball in both hands, swing left leg up high in front, pass the ball under it and go back to a standing position. Raise the right leg, pass the ball under it etc.	Two series of 12, after the first series 10 seconds break	Later: 2 x 15 and 2 x 20
Side straddle, forward bends and pass the ball through your legs with both hands as far as possible, then lift the ball with outstretched arms over your head, spring back.	Two series of 10, after the first series 10 seconds break	Later: 2 x 15 and 2 x 20
On your stomach. Arms and legs stretched out, ball in both hands. Try to lift the ball as high as possible. Spring back.	Two series of 10, after the first series 10 seconds break	Later: 2 x 15 and 2 x 20
On your back. Arms and legs stretched, ball pinned between your feet. Slowly raise your stretched legs, lower them again.	Two series of 10, after the first series 10 seconds break	Later: 2 x 15 and 2 x 20
Partial side straddle. Hold the ball up high, bend backwards, drop the ball, turn your upper body to catch the bouncing ball. In doing so your feet stay on the ground all the time.	Two series of 10, after the first series 10 seconds break	Later: 2 x 15 and 2 x 20
Crouch, ball held in both hands, on the ground, frog jump.	Two series of 12, after the first series 10 seconds break	Later: 2 x 15 and 2 x 20

Game-technical exercises

In order to improve reaction ability, anticipation, orientation and jumping power we include - in addition to purely technical exercises - one or more complex exercises in every training. These are very load intensive, but not so much intended to be exercises for physical improvement. The emphasis is on good execution (catching the ball). These exercises can also be used as speed exercises in which the players work under time pressure within short periods (e.g. 1 minute).

Exercise 1: Dive. The coach places six or seven medicine balls in a semi-circle and places himself at the 11 metre mark with the same number of balls. At a signal the goalkeeper sprints from the centre of his goal to the first medicine ball. As he dashes back, the coach throws the ball which the goalkeeper dives to get. Get back in position, sprint to medicine ball etc. In fitness training and speed training the goalkeeper tries to carry out the exercise as quickly as possible with all seven medicine balls. The balls are thrown in a fast sequence (measure the time).

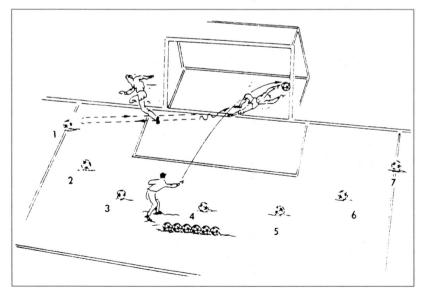

Exercise 2: This exercise is based on a different game situation. The goalkeeper runs out, but is surprised by a lob. The coach positions himself with a few balls at the 11 metre mark. The moment the coach takes the ball in his hand the goalkeeper runs towards the coach. As soon as the coach tries to throw, the goalkeeper starts to run backwards to catch the ball, divert it or tip it over the goal. We repeat this 4 or 5 times.

To start with the coach throws in such a way that the goalkeeper - running backwards - can reach the ball with a relatively well executed jump. Then we can either increase the distance between the coach and the goal or make the throw harder. Fitness or speed training: Running backwards and forwards, in combination with a jump from a backwards dash is very difficult and load intensive. Even if the goalkeeper is to work under time pressure you must make sure that the ball is thrown in such a way that the goalkeeper can reach it.

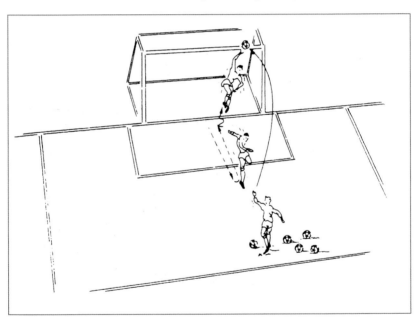

Exercise 3: This exercise is somewhat more diverse because here too tasks must be executed in as short a time as possible and technically correctly. The coach positions himself with 5, 6 balls on the penalty line. Furthermore he places two balls in the corners of the goal area.

Even better though would be to have the balls rolled to these positions by a helper which would make the exercise more realistic. In addition we place a medicine ball in the centre between the two balls. At a signal the goalkeeper dashes to the ball indicated to him (right or left) and dives to get possession of it, puts it down again and dashes around the medicine ball towards the coach. The latter then throws a ball which the goalkeeper jumps to catch. Back to the goal and repeat. Also use it as a fitness exercise.

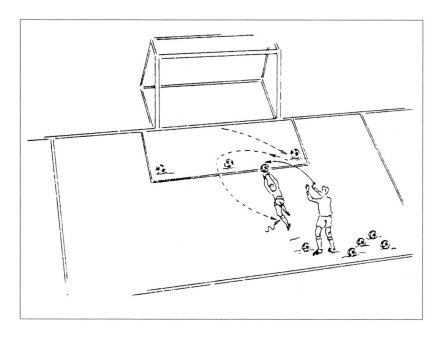

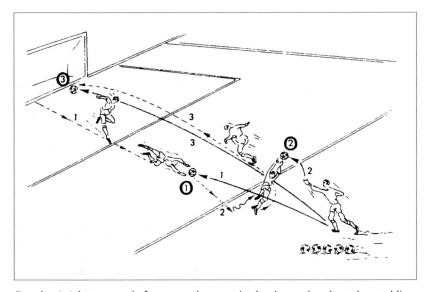

Exercise 4: A last example for a complex exercise begins and ends at the goal line. The coach just needs enough balls and both participants - coach and goalkeeper - must see and play. This exercise is really about a small course for the goalkeeper composed of a number of game elements. The goalkeeper stands on the goal line while the coach waits ready about 20 m away in order to serve the balls. He shoots the first ball at the 11 metre position.

The goalkeeper dashes and throws himself after the ball (1). Throw the ball back and dash to the coach (2) who gets ready to kick a lob and directly afterwards shoots a third ball at the goal (3) in such a way that the goalkeeper can win the ball before the goal line with a powerful dash and a dive.

The degree of difficulty of the exercise can be increased by shooting the first ball in any direction - the goalkeeper must react - and also shooting the second in a direction which is not predetermined. Nevertheless, make sure the height of the ball is such that the goalkeeper can reach it. Also good as a speed exercise (1 minute).

Organisation of defence and game technical exercises

In addition to catching balls the activities of the goalkeeper are very varied. As the most important defence player he must have the tactical equipment of the defender. From a tactical point of view his positional play, running out, directing the wall in the case of free kicks and organising the defence can decide the game. Added to this is that he often joins the attack as the first man and makes the first build-up pass. The positioning of the defenders when there are corners, in order to catch these (to win them, tip them over the goal etc.), are some of his tactical responsibilities.

POSITIONAL PLAY

Good positional play and the shortening of the opponent's shooting angle which it determines is just as important for the goalkeeper as his purely technical qualities. The better he chooses the right angle and the more he shortens the shooting angle of the opponent, the greater chance he has of getting the ball. On the other hand, whenever he goes out he always has to watch out for lobs. The selection of the right angle - that is the centre point between the attacker with the ball and the two posts - is a skill which can only be learnt through frequent practice. In any case it is impossible for a goalkeeper to form a triangle in his mind each time in order to figure out where he should stand. For this we as coaches have a very simple method: we make the imaginary line visible by using a long rubber rope whose two ends we tie to the goal posts. By tensing the rubber rope with his hips the coach forms a sharp angle to the post and can move to the left or right as he likes, while he shoots balls at the goalkeeper. Thanks to the two ropes the latter can choose the right angle without any problem. With regular practice the goalkeeper thus develops automatisms. While we work with one of the goalkeepers on these tasks, the second goalkeeper trains his reaction ability. Example: Run easily with the ball, throw the

ball up, forward roll, stand up and catch the ball. Try to keep the throwing height as low as possible. Of course we cannot always work with the rubber rope, it is also not there in a game. But it is a good start to carry out similar exercises without aids.

The exercise which now follows is, from a game-technical point of view, especially suitable for the orientation of the goalkeeper in positional play (according to the speed of the ball).

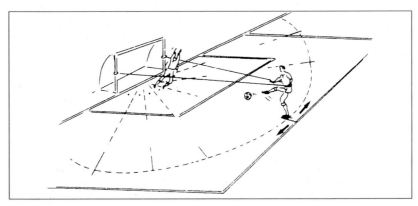

Exercise 1: 4 or 5 players spread themselves over the entire width of the field, supplied with the necessary balls. In the first two series the ball is shot in the sequence 1 to 5. The goalkeeper goes into position and holds. Afterwards free kicks, which is already considerably more difficult. Then we also get the goalkeeper to reduce the shooting angle (running out); after that the tempo of the final sequence is increased.

If you really want to carry out a difficult exercise, then place a goal in the middle of the field and put four to six players around the goal. It should be interesting to watch your goalkeeper.

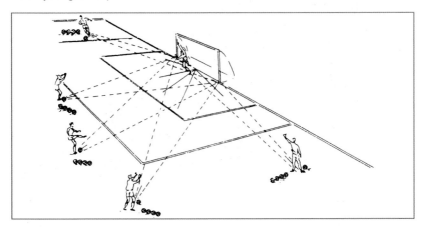

Exercise 2: Reaction exercise. The second goalkeeper stands with his back to a partner who throws him balls. At a signal turn around and catch the ball. The first series high, afterwards low and then alternating freely. Fight for every ball.

This exercise was created from a game phase (corner ball) in which the ball can come from various directions without warning. Example: Short corner. In the case of "normal" opposing attacks it is also important that the goalkeeper can calculate the proper angle in order to have the greatest success in getting the ball.

The goalkeeper must organise the defence in such a way that no opponent can stand before him without being covered. At the same time he must recognise the directions from which danger could come and he must know when he must run out of the goal. Responsible running out of the goal is part of good positional play. In this way the goalkeeper can stop opposing attacks. When should he run out then? Here the laws of defence apply again: when we are sure, we attack. Once this decision has been made, it must be consistently carried out, for the slightest hesitation is usually at the expense of the goalkeeper.

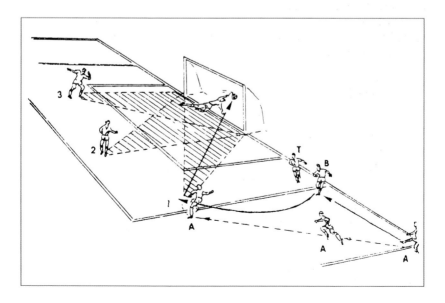

Exercise 1: A preparatory exercise to practise running out. The coach runs towards the goalkeeper with the ball in his hands. The goalkeeper comes out to meet him. Now the ball is thrown, but first with a warning: left, right, high etc. Afterwards freely and more difficult

Exercise 2: The goalkeeper stands on the goal line. The passes are played into the penalty area, a player sprints in. The goalkeeper runs out and wins the through-ball. Gradually lay the ball on more difficultly and harder and at the same time vary direction, not only directly in front of the goal. Finally the kicks are in such a way that the goalkeeper must make a decision whether or not to go out. If he does not go out, then he tries to shorten the angle in order to prevent the attacker from finishing successfully. Therefore vary the passes.

Exercise 3: The second goalkeeper runs next to a helper who throws the ball up high diagonally. The goalkeeper starts, followed by the helper, and catches the ball while the helper tries to head. Another element in running out is the confrontation with an opponent who has the ball at his foot. Unlike fighting for a through ball, here the goalkeeper must not only watch the ball, but at the same time the man who controls the ball. Experience and self-confidence play a major role here. Here all we can say is: lots of training.

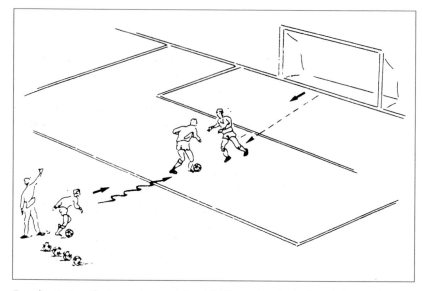

Exercise 4: As a first exercise we take dribbling with the ball and the coming out of the goalkeeper to shorten the angle. The attacker tries to play around the goalkeeper.

Exercise 5: The same exercise, but now the attacker tries to play a lob.

Exercise 6: The initiative is with the goalkeeper: he tries to force the attacker away or executes a deceptive manoeuvre with which he can provoke a predictable reaction by the opponent.

Exercise 7: At speed. The goalkeeper tries to outwit the attacker with a simple body feint (pretends to expose one side by seemingly going to the other side).

The organisation of the defence

We have already discussed the organisational responsibilities of the goalkeeper in the game. But in the case of free kicks too the initiative lies with the goalkeeper. When there is a free kick it is his task to organise his team-mates in such a way that the danger of a goal is reduced as far as possible. Let us take the formation of a wall against a free kick. We often see how goals occur as a result of insufficient organisation in such a situation.

At the moment when the referee whistles it is no use starting a discussion. The goalkeeper organises his players immediately!

Because you have little time the wall is created immediately, possibly too close to the ball, in order to win more time. The two wingers stand facing the goalkeeper and follow his instructions in order to be correctly positioned in a closed line as quickly as possible. Train well in order to react without losing time in games.

For corner balls the same rules apply. The goalkeeper organises his team-mates. Is the classical defence system in place: a man at each post, good headers among the opponents covered etc.? Where is the goalkeeper positioned? At the second post because he can dash forwards more easily than backwards. When does he go out (e.g. centre to the first post), and if he does not go out: what does he do in the next phase?

These are many things which must be thought of in a very short time. If the goalkeeper goes out to win the ball, then everything is on his shoulders: success or failure of his action often decide the goal scoring success of the opponent. The goalkeeper has the loneliest task defending an 11 metres penalty. Here he alone must decide what he should do. Frequent training, including with your own 11 metre specialist, is very useful here. Reserve a few minutes in every training for this.

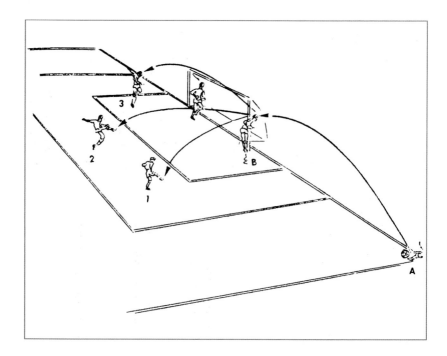

	Pre-season	High-season	Build up	Maintaining standard
	Preparation — General / Specific	Goalkeeper and points game training		
	July · Aug. · Sept.	Oct. · Nov. · Dec. · Jan. · Feb.	March · Apr.	May · June

Fitness build up - Mobility
- Agility
- Speed ability
- Jumping power
- Reaction Ability
- Strength
- Endurance

Basic technique - Various techniques
- Position
- Positional play

Competition technique
- Complex Exercises
- Automatisms

Game-tactics - defence
- Attack
- Organisation of Defence
- Playing system

Training Session 34: Combination Game

Automatisms can only be developed by regularly repeating action sequences. A number of frequently occurring game moves form the basis of our training today. The objective of these moves is to bring a team-mate into the game. The initiative here can go from the person with the ball, but also from the person who calls for the ball. If the initiative comes from the person with the ball, then he determines the further development of the game. If the initiative comes from a team-mate by calling for the ball (e.g. by dashing into the free area), he provides the person with the ball with an obvious solution. He "marches" and the person with the ball passes to him. Both courses of action have the same objective: use a pass to penetrate the opponents area. The most important thing is always that the team-mates offer themselves and run around freely so they can be played to.

Warm-up

Because the entire training is carried out with the ball we have developed the warm-up exercises correspondingly. On the shorter sides of a rectangle 15 m x 25 m six groups form up in such a way that on each side three groups stand opposite each other in rows. Groups opposite each other work together. We need three balls. Each group consists of two or three players. If you have a greater number of players then it is best to divide them into 12 or 16 groups and use the four sides of the square (25 x 25 m), whereby the two groups standing opposite each other always work together. At a signal the first player in line of each group starts. The groups on one side have the ball. In the centre the ball is handed over according to the instructions, the players run on to the other side and go to the back of the line after those with the ball have given the ball to the next person.
- Run with the ball at your feet - play the ball to the other person's foot.
- Move the ball, alternately with the left and right foot - leave the ball standing.

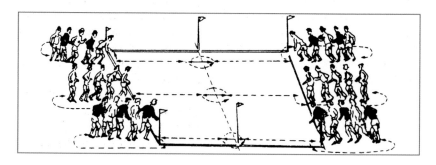

- While running pass the ball around your body.
- While running bounce the ball.
- While walking throw the ball up high and receive it with your foot.
- Short pass and change of pace.
- Move the ball, go past the player coming towards you, turn and play the ball back.
- Throw the ball up high and jump to catch it.
- Roll the ball along the ground with your hands.
- Pass in the centre - both dash towards the ball.
- Roll the ball to the centre - both players dash to it.
- At speed to the centre with the ball at your feet.
- Move the ball at speed, after 7 m pass and sprint to the end.

Main part

We divide the players into groups of four for the training. Because the emphasis is on game moves, the number of repetitions focusing on technical execution will be limited. Because the players first execute each exercise technically cleanly, at the same time they learn the content of the exercise.

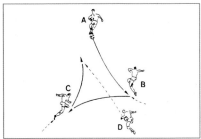
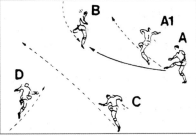

Exercise 1:
Pass to a predetermined player. Choosing the team-mate and running free are made easier by "numbering" the players (A, B, C, D). If Player A has the ball, then B knows that he must run free. Gradually increase the pace.

Exercise 2:
Play the pass and sprint away. Now A gives the pass to B, who is running freely, and A now dashes into the free area (as preparation for later exercise).
- Try to find out up how far a group can increase its pace.
- Try to hide the running free (of the ball recipient) as long as possible.
- Try to hide the moment of play-off as far as possible. First a body feint, then play.

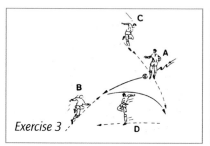

Exercise 3

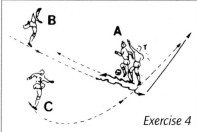

Exercise 4

Exercise 3: Playing freely. Players A and B carry out a pretended manoeuvre in order to give player C a chance to run free: Player A passes to B. Meanwhile D makes room (creates a free space) so that player C can run free. Player C runs free the moment A and B start their pretended action (Player B knows what C will do).

Exercise 4: Break through with the help of a shielded player, player A - in ball possession - is covered by opponent T who does not directly attack the person with the ball, but rather prevents him from penetrating further forwards. Player A is thus forced to play off to the side. Player B comes to a his help, while C waits in readiness. The moment B runs past him, player A leaves the ball standing for B while C dashes into the depth of the field. Player B takes over the ball and plays to C further upfield.

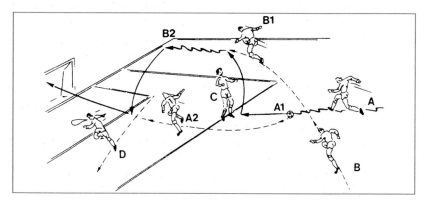

Exercise 5: Intersect each other - play to a midfield player on the outside line. Player A forces his way into the centre. Midfield player B runs free on the outside line while A plays to player C who directly plays on to player B. Player A stops briefly. As soon as B is at the ball, D makes room in the centre (draws opponent with them), then A dashes in and receives the pass from B.

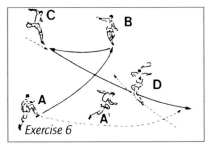

Exercise 6

Exercise 7

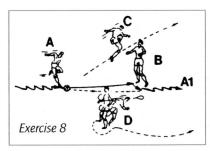

Exercise 8

Exercise 6: Play the ball in a cross - involve the winger in play in midfield. Midfield player A - in possession - moves up along the outside line, passes to B and stays "calm". Player B plays back to C, whereupon winger D leaves the outside line and calls for the ball. Free space has been created: On the outside line C plays the ball upfield, to where A has already rushed. With both moves it is important that the timing is right and the most important intentions are hidden. Even supposedly unimportant actions (player who calls for the ball and doesn't get it creates free space) must be well practised.

Exercise 7: By forming a defensive shield between the player to be passed to and the opposing player a passing opportunity is created. Player A passes to C and player diagonally goes to the front where he calls to have the ball returned to him. Meanwhile player B starts at the same time, and D makes room for A as he dashes up. Player C pretends to play the ball to A, but gives it to B, who moves up.

Exercise 8: Close to the goal we can use the same move in order to immediately shoot at the goal. Exercise 8 is a variant. Here C and D draw attention to themselves while A passes to C. C pretends that he is going to play to D, but stops the ball for A, who comes up behind B and immediately shoots or plays on himself.

Training Session 35: Fitness Training: Speed Ability

When we carry out a training with the ball we can place the emphasis in various ways which means that one and the same exercise can be executed differently and at the same time has a different objective. We can put the emphasis on execution, i.e. accuracy and timing. Here speed takes second place. We can put the emphasis on fast handling of the ball or on the speed with which a player changes his position: playing without the ball. Finally, with regard to game technique we can combine the various aspects and thus come as close as possible to the real game situation. Then we pay attention to all the points mentioned. In such a competition-like exercise the intention must remain hidden as long as possible. Make sure that the players do not offer themselves too early because they know what will happen. They must wait as long as possible and then suddenly accelerate or play an appropriate pass. If you pay particular attention to this and bring more points game atmosphere into the exercises, you as coach are working on your players' mentality. In the training which now follows the accent is on the pace and assertive ability. In addition to balls, 10 flagpoles are needed, some hurdles and a few cones. We have incorporated a load test in the exercises.

Warm-up

Organisation: in rows of two across the width of the field.
• Run around to loosen up.
• Walk, alternately large and small steps, roll off the foot well, from the heel to the toes.
• Run around to loosen up - at a signal run on the spot - half raise your knee (25 times), run 20 m and again run on the spot.
• Run to loosen up, at a signal go into a crouch and spring back twice.
• Walk, at every third step swing your leg up forwards as high as possible and touch your foot with both hands.
• Run to loosen up, while running turn your torso and look at your heel (left and right).
• Run sideways, left and right.
• Walk - swing your arms in circles forwards and backwards.
• Run two metres backwards, half turn, run on etc.
• Walk, at a signal stop, bend forwards, backwards, left and right. Then circle your head around to the left and right.
• Run to loosen up - at a signal run on the spot, systematically increase the pace.
• Run to loosen up - at a signal increase the pace to short sprints (six or seven times).
• Run backwards - at a signal turn and accelerate briefly.
• Sprint over the entire width of the field.
• Run to loosen up and breathe deeply.

Main part

We divide the players into groups of six who work together, against each other or individually during the entire training.

FIRST SERIES

The groups of six are further divided into groups of three. Each carries out both exercises (change over).

Exercise 1: Moving the ball and running hurdles. Three players. The following are required: three hurdles and three balls. Play the ball under the hurdles while the player jumps over the hurdle. Get the ball under control and go to the next hurdle. The next players follow at short intervals. As soon as they have reached the other end they take the ball at speed around the hurdles back to the starting position. Immediately repeat, but now the second player takes the lead (the leader thus has a longer break each time). After three rounds a have a 15 seconds break, then the exercise is repeated three times.

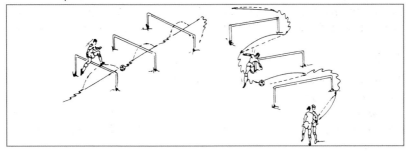

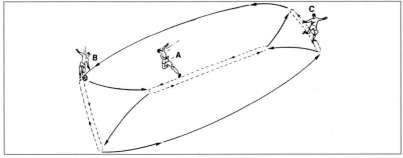

Exercise 2: Wall pass mill. Three players, 1 ball. Player A sprints up and back again, to alternately play a wall pass with B and C. After a long pass from Player B to C, B dashes back to the starting position while A sprints to C for a wall pass. Regularly change over.

SECOND SERIES

Exercise 1: Play off and run free. Three players, 1 ball. Player A positions himself with Player B 25 m away from C. A takes the ball 5 m towards C and plays the ball steeply to B as he sprints up, while A then immediately dashes off to the right to receive the pass from B. B dashes back to the starting position and A moves the ball at a high pace to C, gives him the ball and joins up behind him. The exercise is now carried out with player C towards B (continuously).

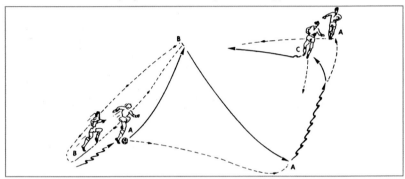

Exercise 2: The three other players have used the fence around the field to carry out various exercises:
- Sprint to the post after the next one - run two lengths easily, etc.
- Sprint three posts forwards - one length back.
- Run backwards - run two lengths forwards.
- Jump: over the railing and back between two posts.
- Crawl: under the railing and back.
- Combinations: Jump over the fence and come back underneath it. Further combinations with sprints and jumps.

THIRD SERIES

Kilometre test in groups of three, one after the other. This running test is excellently suited to testing fitness. Note the times of all players and compare them regularly. 3 players always run at once. From starting position 1 to post 2 and back to 1 again, then to 3, until 7. Carry out 2 rounds in a row in this way (also cf. Training session 16). Then group 2 starts while group 3 actively recover.

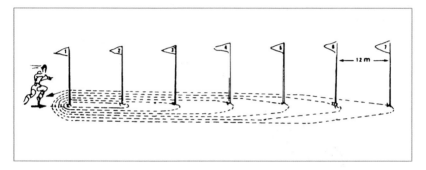

FOURTH SERIES

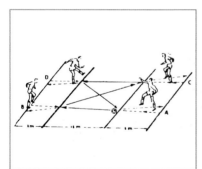

Exercise 1: Accordion game. Four players and a ball. The players form up in pairs at a distance of 25 m apart. The ball is 5 m in front of player A who begins. The ball is played backwards and forwards in such a way that the player who is passed to runs towards the ball, passes and immediately runs back to take his place again. Gradually increase the pace. Variants (more strenuous): Both players standing opposite the person with the ball run forwards to receive the pass. The players who notices that the pass is not meant for him turns away and runs back to his position. The person with the ball, however, now no longer passes the ball evenly, but rather "normally", very short (even only 50 cm) or very long (more difficult because received while running hard). No matter what happens the two players must dash for the ball. Regularly two players swap with the other two players in the group, meanwhile carry out the next exercise.

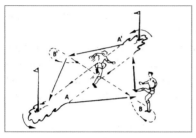

Exercise 2: Double wall pass. Player A moves the ball around the flagpoles, passes to B who offers himself and lets the ball bounce back into the path of A. B immediately dashes to the opposite side while A moves the ball around the poles and gets ready for the next wall pass.

FIFTH SERIES

During the competition period we must not forget smaller or bigger practice games in training. Do not just let two groups "kick around", but organise games with a particular objective. Here is a game 3 against 3. The rules: A maximum of three passes when in possession of the ball. Other rules could be:
- The ball must be played on directly.
- A goal is only valid if a certain player has been involved in the game.

SIXTH SERIES

Play off and run after the ball. Players form up e.g. around the centre circle. The person with the ball plays the ball into the centre and runs after it. The player in the centre immediately passes to the next player and runs after the pass. This player (B) in turn passes into the centre (now A) and runs after it etc. Continuously and systematically increase the pace.

Two annoyances which regularly occur in the winter period are the bad condition of the pitch (hard or soggy) and blisters. Here are some tips.

Pitch: In addition to the proper choice of sprigs there is another way of preventing lumps of mud and snow building up under your boots. We rub - a day before is best - an old fashioned substance into the soles of the boots, namely soot. Let them dry well. This protective layer keeps off mud and snow so that the soles remain free.

Blisters: You can try to prevent blisters by putting talcum in your socks. If a player gets blisters, which is often very painful, then you can ease the pain by putting a bandage of gauze and plaster on it (several mm thick) in such a way that a ring is placed around the blister which eases the pressure (and the pain).

Training Session 36: Seeing and Offering Oneself

Today's topic "seeing and offering oneself" is basically about cleanly and accurately passing on the ball. The initiative here can come from the person with the ball (seeing) or from someone without the ball (offering oneself). Seeing and offering oneself are not only elements of a game move, but must be expressed in the attitude of the entire team during a game. This team must try to develop a kind of dynamic radiation. After the warm-up we begin with the main part whereby the ball is at the centre of attention.

Main part

IN PAIRS WITH A BALL

Exercise 1: The players run up next to each other at a certain distance. The player without the ball dashes forwards and has the ball played into his path. Variant: The initiative comes from the person with the ball: pass and the team-mate dashes.

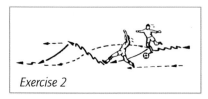

Exercise 2

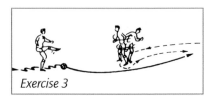

Exercise 3

Exercise 4

Exercise 2: Intersect. The player without the ball runs away free and get the ball passed into his path. Make sure that the players do not run too far ahead in a straight line but change direction in time and intersect each other. Try to make this exercise as realistic as possible. Never play the ball and intersect at the same pace, instead seek a free area by expressly changing pace.

Exercise 3: Getting away from an (imaginary) opponent. Both players run towards each other. The player offering himself does not run too quickly (draws the opponent with him). Suddenly he gets away with a fast turn and dashes into the free area where he kicks the pass.

Exercise 4: Wall pass. In this exercise, offering oneself plays a decisive role. Suddenly passing on the ball with a just as surprising change of pace in order to receive the ball further up field is a school book example of teamwork. Put the accent on the suddenness and thus the surprising element in the exercise: change of pace.

IN PAIRS WITH AN OPPONENT

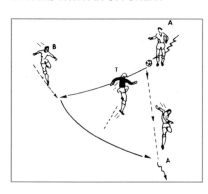

In a game it often happens that two players stand opposite an opponent. This is a situation for the wall pass. We must practise this - with an opponent - as often as possible. It is important that we pay attention to changing the pace and hiding our intention as long as possible. Let the opponent decide himself as well: whether to go along or not. Pay attention to the solutions which the players find.

Exercise 1

Exercise 2

Exercise 1: Offering. The player without the ball and moves in such a way that he can be passed to. The defender attacks the person with the ball or stops him playing off. Make frequent use of changes of pace. Regularly change the defenders.
Variant 1: The person with the ball draws the defender towards himself or runs towards him.
Variant 2: The team-mate shakes off the opponent.

Exercise 2: Bringing midfield players into the game. A moves the ball towards the defenders while the team mate moving up moves in such a way (e.g. intersecting behind the person with the ball) that he can be played to or, better still, brought into the game. After a few prescribed game moves let the players practise freely. Nevertheless, ensure changes of pace.

IN THREES WITH OPPONENT (3:1)

Exercise 1: Have the players play freely, but in such a way that the two free team-mates can be played to each time. Despite numerical superiority always keep moving. Game rule: touch the ball twice and immediately play on etc.

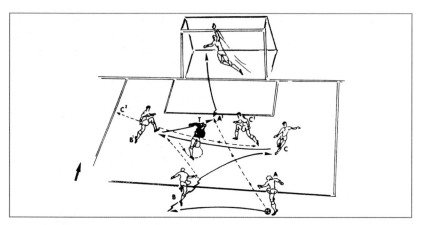

Exercise 2: Player A plays across the width to B who moves up and plays a wall pass with C. C follows the ball and this clears the way for A who suddenly offers himself further up while player C calls for the ball. A shoots at goal or plays into the path of C who shoots at goal. Keep an eye on the timing and involve every player in the game. Afterwards let the players combine freely within the framework of their exercise task.

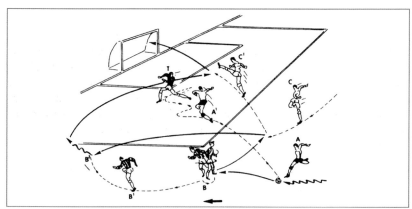

Exercise 3: In this exercise the attack along the outside line is built up. Midfield player A moves up and passes to winger B. He passes back to C while B suddenly turns around, dashes upfield along the outside line and then has the ball played to him by C. Meanwhile A has moved up - directly towards opponent T - and calls for the ball. By doing so he clears the way for C who has held back after passing to B. C runs to the through-ball from B and shoots at the goal.

These exercises have the task of developing certain automatisms in the players and even more in the player groups. Let the players begin simply, e.g. by involving an opponent. Everything works of course, until a second defender is added. Then the ideas of the players count more. The exercise is then more like a genuine game situation and elements such as surprise, shaking off, or seeing and playing are used more and more. The defenders also try to find solutions for their problems, e.g. with area marking.

GAME

At the end we organise a game in which the emphasis is on active orientation and playing. Game rules: Do not run with the ball at your foot - involve team-mates in the game. Initially the initiative is with the person with the ball. He passes into the free area and a team-mate reacts to this pass. Then the person with the ball moves the ball until a team-mate offers himself. The initiative is then with the team-mate and not with the person with the ball. Play is on a field 20 m x 40 m with two small goals.

Training Session 37: Fitness Training in Pairs

Certain forms of training particularly appeal to players. These include partner exercises. If you let the players do what they want, however, then they usually choose a training partner who "suits" them. The less active players then also seek a corresponding player which is not so good for developing activity. Therefore give the players the tasks they would normally have in the team (forward with midfield player, midfield player with defender etc.). If you let the groups play against each other in certain exercises then you can assume that they will all put in the greatest effort. This is also the case when you let players carry out exercises freely in small groups in which a group must sprint after the (constantly changing) leader as closely as possible. You can also use partner exercises to achieve very high a physical loads.

Warm-up

We get the players to work in pairs for the warm-up too. Have the pairs run freely across the field. Apart from generally developing exercises we can get the players to dash, run in snaking lines (while constantly overtaking each other), and with varying

pace as well as jumping and carrying exercises. At the same time you can orientate the warm-up to the actual training and include a few preparatory exercises. Examples:
- One player runs backwards, the second forwards. A dashes past B, player B turns round and runs after him etc.

- The player running backwards tries to force player A away with delaying movements (feigned movements).

In addition we get the players to work freely for several minutes (five to seven minutes). Only give the players a few tips:
- Arm and leg exercises
- Sudden changes of direction
- Sudden change of pace
- Combinations and
- Shaking off the pursuer (with all means).
Change over every 30 seconds. Right from the start an active atmosphere is created which helps the rest of the training. The coach must always observe attentively, however, especially those pairs which move off to distant corners in order to take it a little more easily.

Main part

The pairs remain together during the whole training. The training is finished with a practice game with two groups of four. We begin with a number of very simple exercises in which one player works in each case (5 times, then swap roles).

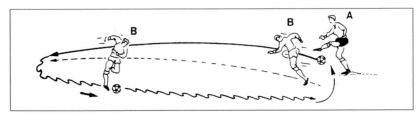

Exercise 1: Players A and B stand next to each other. Player A plays the ball about 15 m forwards, B dashes after it, gets the ball under control and comes back as quickly as possible with the ball at his foot. Variant: B dashes off and calls for the ball, A passes (not too low).

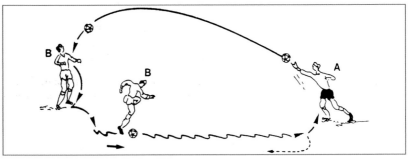

Exercise 2: Ball reception and change of position. The players stand 10 to 15 m apart. Player A throws or lobs the ball to B, who receives the ball (chest, head) and then quickly moves it to A. In the meantime A sprints into B's place (change of position), and then B throws (continuously).

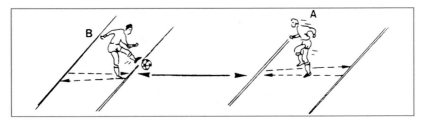

Exercise 3: Accordion. Both players stand opposite each other about 10 to 15 m apart. Player A plays the ball to B who runs towards the ball, directly passes it back and runs back to the starting position as quickly as possible. Meanwhile A has dashed to the ball again, and A passes and runs back backwards (continuously).

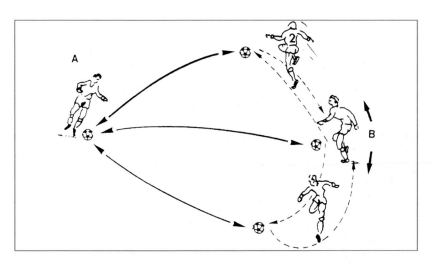

Exercise 4: Returning the ball. Player A plays the ball in various directions, B runs to get the ball and plays it back directly from a hard run. Regularly swap positions.

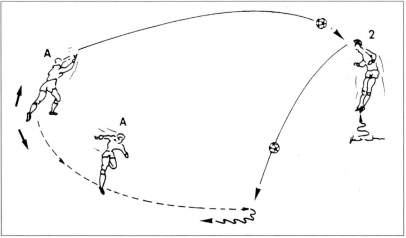

Exercise 5: Heading pass. Player A throws the ball to B who extends the pass with his head, either in a direction chosen himself or in a direction indicated by Player A. A dashes, gets the ball and dribbles back to the starting position.

Exercise 6: Pass - acceleration. The two players stand 25 m opposite each other with a ball each. They move the balls towards each other and pass upfield (pass for partner), then they turn round and try to get the ball under control as quickly as possible. Back to starting point (continuously).

Exercise 7: Pass with change of direction. A variant of the previous exercise is not to play the ball upfield, but instead to the left or right and with a dash to get the partner's pass under control.

If we want to put the emphasis more on the distance to be run, we can mark the course with flagpoles. This stops the players increasingly shortening the running distances in the exercises. This also applies to the previous exercises. We can also involve the poles in the exercises.

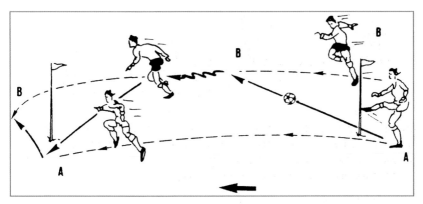

Exercise 8: Pass - acceleration. Two players form up to the right and left of a flagpole. Player A passes diagonally to player B who then runs to get the ball. Player B gets the ball under control and quickly moves it on while A dashes to the second pole and receives the pass. A gives the ball to B behind the flagpole, and now B begins.

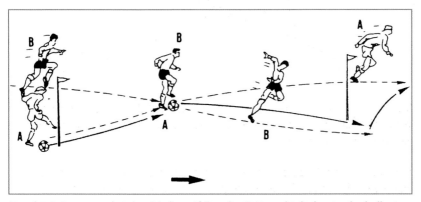

Exercise 9: Pass - acceleration. Variant of Exercise 8. B again dashes to the ball, stops it, leaves the ball standing for A and dashes on. Meanwhile A has run to the ball and passes into the path of B while he himself dashed to the other side of the pole.

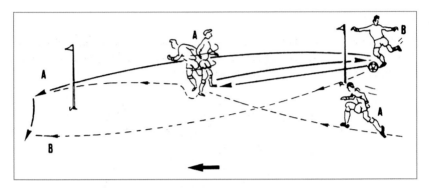

Exercise 10: Pass - acceleration. At the beginning the same formation as in Exercise 8. Player A dashes diagonally into the pass from B. A directly plays back to B with a long pass plays the ball towards the second pole, to which A dashes. After making the long pass B sprints to the second pole.

Training Session 38: Training Teamwork

Because the ball is faster than the player and it never gets tired, we try to let the ball go. Once in possession we must therefore seek a free team-mate and pass to him. The moment we receive the ball a team-mate must move and run free so that we can play the pass. In order to practise this we have developed a training which consists of a circuit with three stations. These are: A four field game (1), soccer tennis (2) and soccer with three groups (3). Beforehand we carry out a warm-up.

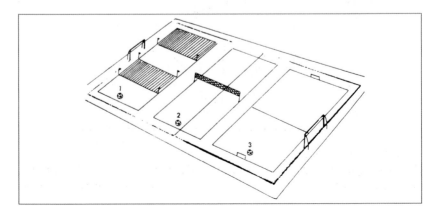

Main part

The emphasis is on grasping situations and accuracy of passes. Players divide up into three groups which each in turn divide into two groups. They play 16 minutes at each station then move to the next (each game twice).

Exercise 1: Four field game. Each team has two fields which do not a border on each other. They can position themselves freely in one of the two fields, to change fields, however, they may not cross the opponents field (go round the outside). At least two players must remain in each field. Game idea: Try to play the ball between your own fields (shifting the game), without the opponent getting the ball. If the ball is played out, then it goes to the opponent.

Exercise 2: Soccer tennis.
Here the emphasis is on good observation of the game and the right positioning of the team-mates. Each team may only touch the ball three times at the most

before it is played back into the other field. Any team which has scored a point serves (kick-off or throw-in).

Difficult variants:
- Play freely and each time let the ball bounce once
- Only play with your head (foot)
- After playing off the player dashes to a position outside his field.

Exercise 3: Game with three teams. Here not only accurate play plays a role, but also reaction speed and rapid switching from attack to defence when the ball is lost. This applies especially to the third team which always supports the team with the ball. If the ball is gained, then this team immediately switches to join the attack of the team which now has the ball. And watch out: In defence you always play with numerical minority so that both area and man marking (player with the ball) are necessary.

Training Session 39: Fitness Training

In fitness training there are always some players who try shirk. There are of course a number of ways of dealing with this, but instead of walking around with a whip we can just as easily create conditions under which everybody has the same load. Possibilities which we have already used are: group game, group competitions etc., whereby every player uses all his strength in order to get a good result for the group. Another possibility is to get the groups to practise under load without an accountable final result arising. Here the player does not want to seem as if he can't stand the pace up, and will orient himself towards the efforts of the others.

Today's very comprehensive training begins on the pitch. There the warm-up can be carried out. In order to increase load, on the way back they do not walk, but run easily. Every player carries out the individual exercises four times each. When the first wave has a third of the distance behind them, the second groups starts etc.

Main part

FIRST SERIES: SPRINTS

Exercise 1: Intensify in three stages until a maximum speed is reached, dash on to the end.

Exercise 2: Accelerate, suddenly a hard acceleration and then gradually slow down.

Exercise 3: Accelerate, slow down and immediately accelerate again until maximum speed is reached.

Exercise 4: Run backwards, half turn - sprint.

Exercise 5: Run backwards, short turn, accelerate with change of pace.

Exercise 6: Sprint against each other over the entire distance.

SECOND SERIES: ACCELERATIONS WITH AGILITY REQUIREMENTS

Here the players start from various starting positions. Start as quickly as possible, accelerate over 10 m, change pace, slow down.

Exercise 1

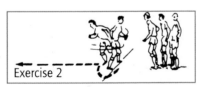

Exercise 2

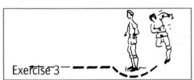

Exercise 3

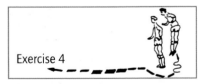

Exercise 4

Exercise 1: Starting position: lying on the back.

Exercise 2: Starting position: start with your back to the course.

Exercise 3: Starting position: stand behind your partner.

Exercise 4: Starting position: stand behind your partner. After a closing jump accelerate.

THIRD SERIES: SPRINTS IN PAIRS

Exercise 1

Exercise 2

Exercise 3

Exercise 4

Exercise 1: Sprints against a partner.

Exercise 2: Run backwards, half turn, carry on running forwards etc.

Exercise 3: Zigzag run. Second man is pursuer.

Exercise 4: Second man runs behind and reacts to all deceptive actions.

This training is finished with three game forms which in an attractive way cause the players to greatly exert themselves.

GAME 1: PARTY BALL GAME ACCORDING TO HANDBALL RULES

Two teams of six to nine players each play against each other on half a field. Two (smaller) balls are needed. The team in ball possession tries to achieve as many passes as possible. No running with the ball in your hands. The team mates must offer themselves in plenty of time. The opposing team tries to intercept ball.

GAME 2: HANDBALL

Handball is a good game to keep the players moving and train area marking. The opponent is not attacked immediately.

Attacking team: rapid passing on of the ball without running while carrying the ball. Build up an attack with changes of position, be prepared for a very fast counter attack of the opponent.

Defending team: go back quickly and cover all attackers without directly intervening. While marking always keep moving and thus provoke a bad pass by the opponent. The emphasis is on rapid passing on of the ball and on running so that the person with the ball finds team-mates who can be played to. Risk long passes to shift the game.

GAME 3: SOCCER

The emphases mentioned for the previous game are now applied to a game of soccer: the ball must be played on quickly and the players make sure that they can be played to. When the ball is lost the players used position-related defence: do not stand in front of the goal but keep moving constantly.

Training Session 40: Game after Load

As a rule the load is gradually increased from exercise to exercise. Today we want to proceed differently for a change. We start with a load intensive part and then let the players carry out a game in order to observe the reactions and the precision of their actions.

Warm-up

We carry out a hard warm-up without the ball, whereby we have the players carry out all elements carefully. We finish the warm-up with a number of long sprints.

Main part

We start with a performance test, namely the Cooper Test: cover as great a distance as possible in 12 minutes. In order to stimulate the fighting spirit right from the start, we have the players start in two groups. The second groups starts after the first has covered about 100 m. After every round call out the time and spur the players on. Which group will cover the greatest distance? At the finish the players immediately check their pulse, again after five minutes. All keep moving (active break: do not sit down or stand still).
For the rest of the training we divide the players into four groups.

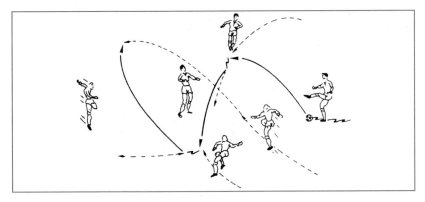

Exercise 1: The ball is passed rapidly within the group, with frequent accelerations and changes of pace. The emphasis is on playing into the path of team-mates.

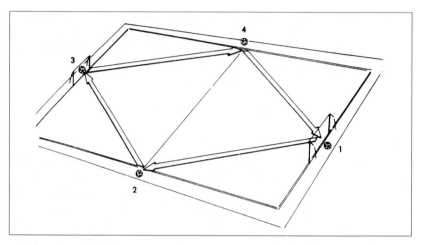

Exercise 2: Passing on game. In this exercise we used the same elements of movement as in the previous exercise but the ball must be moved from one point to the next. Competition between the groups is possible. Hereby the emphasis can be on:

- Rapid concerted action when passing on the ball from one point to another.
- Speed ability (which group will reach the next point first?).

The four groups form up at the positions 1, 2, 3 and 4. Each group has a ball. At a signal they make a concerted move from position to position; each player touches the ball at least twice between two positions. At the target position (for Group 1 it is position 2 etc.) the ball is left standing and the players sprint back in the reverse direction to the starting place in order to begin again with the ball lying there ready. 5, 7 or 10 laps according to instructions.

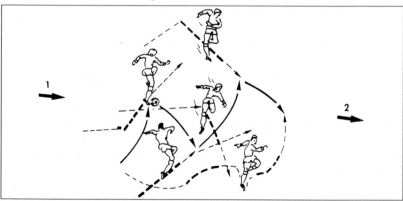

It is recommendable to set the following tasks for the first three rounds: Play the ball on quickly. Then make a concerted move at speed whereby the group which first arrives gets points. If the goalkeepers are involved in this game they may get the ball under control with their hands and throw it to a team-mate.
After this very strenuous exercise follow two game forms.

1ST GAME FORM: SEEKING THE BALL DISTRIBUTOR

Two teams with five or six players each play on a half pitch with small goals. Each team has a ball distributor whom they can either mark (armband) or not (then the opponent must find out who he is). There is no man marking, instead they try to get the opponent out of the game with lots of running work and to get the ball. Here the ball distributor is the key figure. If the ball distributor is played to, one or two players immediately run free. In summary: Rapid passing on of the ball, playing to a particular player, developing goal opportunities and converting them.

2ND GAME FORM: SCORING GOALS FROM THE REAR SIDE

Now the task is varied somewhat. The game task remains the same, but we move the goals 3 m forwards so that a space is created behind the goals. Because goals must be shot from the rear side of the goal, the players are forced to play across the breadth of the field in order to be able to play to someone behind the goal. Each time a player must move up from the second row in order to be able to convert the pass behind the goal. You can also count certain types of goals (e.g. headers) double.

The two other groups (and goalkeepers) take the other goal in order to practise two frequently occurring game situations:
- The wall pass followed by a goal shot,
- Bringing another team-mate into the game on the outside line followed by a return pass in front of the goal.

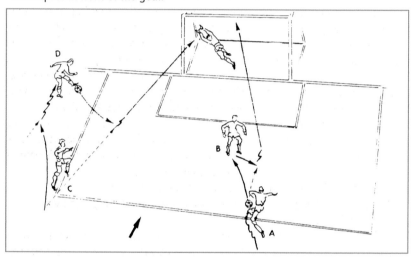

Have these exercises carried out one after the other, i.e. the first group starts with the wall pass, comes back and joins up behind the second group who practise the return pass.

Then the first group does the second exercise etc. After 10 minutes they swap with the groups playing the practice game.

Training Session 41: The Offside Trap

The offside trap is a tactical tool in defence which is used by many teams. It has advantages and disadvantages but certainly a team which uses it must play in a concentrated way for this tactic can go wrong because the offside trap depends on collective involvement of the entire line of defence. The opposing attackers are eliminated through joint and simultaneous moving up of the defence players. This also immediately shows up the weakness. Nobody wants to be the last to take the step forwards and thus possibly be responsible for an opposing goal. Thus everyone is under pressure. As well as this, you'll always have the option of directly eliminating the attacker with an individual action or collectively using the offside trap. Before we learn the use of the offside trap a number of automatisms must be developed with which this can be avoided. The attackers of the front line are hindered in their game by the danger of an offside trap. On the other hand, they can also position themselves directly near the offside trap and profit from its failure because then absolutely no more coverage is possible.

From the second row there are also chances to break through:
- individually: a player pretends he wants to play to a team-mate, but then marches on himself.
- or collectively: pass behind the defence to a player moving up from the midfield or, when one's own defence has moved up extremely far, from one's own defence.

When on the defensive, the players must automatically take over the position of their team-mates, for when the ball is lost the positions must be secured. If the midfield has moved up, the attackers thus take on the tasks of the midfield. If a defender moves up, then his place is taken by another. It is also important that a pass is played accurately because such an attack is concentrated on a single

action. Note: If your opponent is a team which consistently plays using offside, then it is advisable to intentionally run offside at the beginning of the game a few times. In this way the opponent's attentiveness drops.

Main part

After the thorough warm-up we begin with an individual exercise: form up in a line with three parts whereby the players have a gap of 3 m on all sides. The players run in this formation alternately fast and slowly across the length of the field. At a signal the runners in front turn briefly to the left or right. The players running behind them sprint through and the players who turned off join up at the back. Continuously, until everything runs quickly. Repeat this exercise, but now with a change of pace during the dash.

EXERCISE WITHOUT THE BALL

Formation and basic rules are the same as in the previous exercise, but now only one player dashes up (call out the name).
a) the coach determines the player beforehand. At a signal the other players turn off, and the previously determined player sprints on.
b) the coach calls the name of the player who moves up as the late as possible. The other players in this row dash away with a turn.

EXERCISE WITH THE BALL

Exercise 1: Laying the ball on for yourself.
Two lines stand 25 m apart. At a signal the two rows run towards each other,

whereby the "attackers" pass the ball to each other. At a second signal the defenders dash, while the player with the ball plays the ball on for himself and the other attackers turn off so as not to get off side.
When this is mastered,
- give the signal later so that the space between the rows smaller,
- get the person with the ball to pass at the last moment.

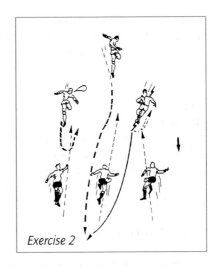

Exercise 2

Afterwards get the players to practise a few times on their own. Attackers keep secret as long as possible which player will lay the ball on for himself.

Exercise 2: Involve team-mates in the game. With the same exercise a team-mate is sent into the area. Again start easily and with plenty of space so that the players have the chance to master the action mentally and technically. Then reduce the area and the time so that more speed ability is called for. Get the players who are moving up to start from well behind the line of attack a few times and get the defenders to move up very quickly. The person with the ball makes a pass at the last moment (or a lob) to the players moving up and then turns away himself. In practice watch out for the goalkeeper running out far.

GAME-TACTICAL EXERCISES

In the previous exercises we have provided for the necessary game-technical foundations. We can now develop the feeling for the game-tactical execution.

Exercise 1

Exercise 1: Game towards a goal. Get the players to freely move in a concerted way, while the coach follows the game and makes the necessary comments. At a signal from the coach the defenders storm forwards. The attackers react. The goalkeeper now also joins in.

Exercise 2: Attack via defenders. Here we again get the players to act freely. The defenders try to stop the attack by moving up in as close a formation as possible in order to close all space to the attackers. These try to get their front spearhead into the game. If that does not work, there is a return pass to the last man (offside trap rule), after which he lays the ball on for himself. The other defenders remain passive (just dash).

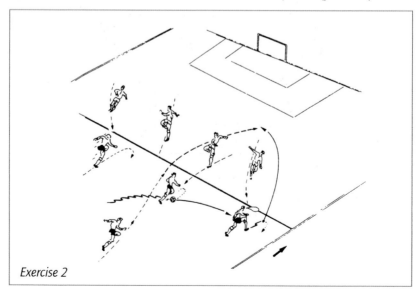

Exercise 2

PRACTICAL GAMES

There is nowhere better to learn than in a practical situations. Therefore we will carry out a few game forms.
1. Game towards a goal. The defenders try to intercept the attacks using the offside trap.

2. Game towards two small goals. On the attack: avoid offside traps. In the defence: use offside traps to let the attack dissipate.

Training Session 42: Running Training with the Ball

In the following training session we will handle a very important aspect: mutual securing. In preparation, today we will carry out a running training with the ball in which the emphasis is on the technical execution. The objective is:
- Improve peripheral vision,
- Improve spatial orientation and anticipation or the feeling for where an object is, how it changes its position and where it will move to (in order to get the object under control),
- The feeling for the position of the midfield player, - The automatic execution of movements.

Warm-up

Once again we choose the proven formation in a square in which the players spread themselves along the four sides and in each case the two opposite groups work together. Get the players to work with the ball (alternately using hands and feet): pass the ball into the centre or throw it to the partner. After this preparation we can move on to the actual training.

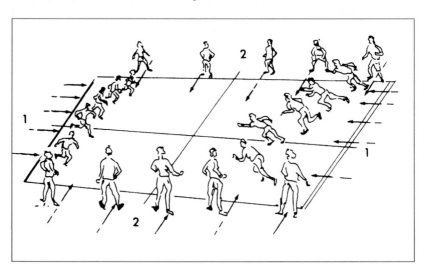

Main part

Exercise 1: Two players pass the ball back and forth while running. Pay attention to the pace and at the right moment cleanly pass the ball into the partners half.
Variant 1: The initiative is with the person with the ball - he calls, and then his partner goes through.
Variant 2: The initiative is with the player without the ball - he calls and goes through whereupon the person with the ball gives the pass. Repeat, but now without a call.

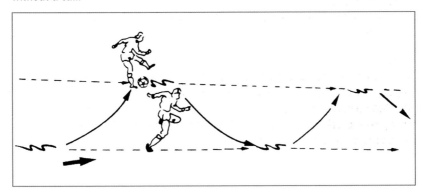

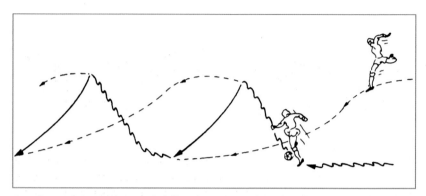

Exercise 2: Change of pace and direction. This task is already a little more difficult because both players intersect each other and then play the ball off from a covered position. The emphasis here is on proper timing, going through without the ball, so that the person with the ball can play the pass. The initiative changes as in the previous exercise.

Exercise 3: Intersecting in pairs, each has a ball. The two players stand 25 m apart. At the signal they run towards each other with the ball at their feet. When they are 5 m apart, they pass to the left and dash off to the right themselves (behind the pass of the partner).
Options:
- Over the last metres with the ball lower the pace, give a clean pass and then dash behind the pass of the team-mate,
- Move the ball towards each other as fast as possible, pass, turn around, lower the pace briefly, then suddenly accelerate,
- Hide the decisive pass and dash as long as possible,
- The pass can be played hard or softly into all corners of the designated zone.

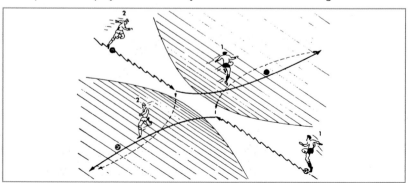

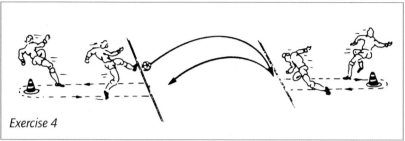

Exercise 4

Exercise 4: Accordion with lob. The two players initially stand 25 m apart. The player with the ball lobs it to his team-mate in such a way that he has to run towards the ball in order to play it back (continuously). Play the ball back to the team-mate to the left and right as well as short and long.

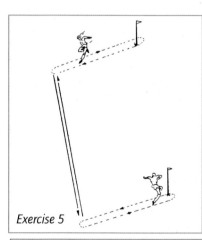

Exercise 5

Exercise 5: Passing and dashing to the sideline. The players stand about 10 m from the sideline (or the flagpole).

Exercise 6: Passing in threes with change of place. The players A, B and C position themselves at three corners of a square (15 m x 15 m). In rapid sequence the ball is played into the currently free corner and the player closest to it dashes to the ball while the player who made the pass takes up the position which has become free.

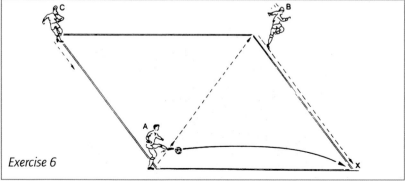

Exercise 6

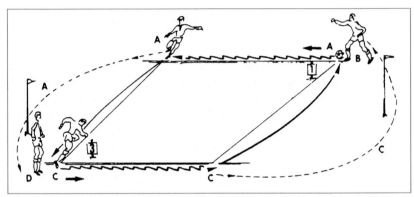

Exercise 7: Passing in fours with a change of place. A and B at position 1, C and D at position 3. Player A starts with the ball from position 1 and passes to C at Position 3, sprints on (around the flagpole) and takes up his place behind D. Meanwhile C has dribbled to position 4, passes to B and sprints around the other flagpole to position 1 (continuously).

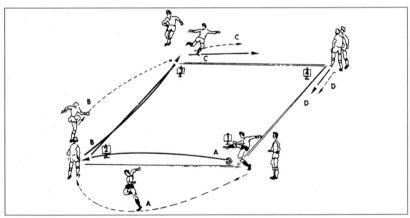

Exercise 8: Passing in groups of eight with change of place. We use the same square (an even bigger one is better), at each corner of which two players position themselves. Player A starts from position 1 by making a pass to B (position 2) and then sprinting in an arc to position 2 (always run after the ball). Player B plays the ball on and also follows it. Continuous. Carry out quickly, the players must keep their wits about them, however, and kick powerful passes. Variant: Player A passes to position 2. B's team-mate plays the ball on directly to player B as he dashes off etc. When training is over, pass the ball to each other easily.

Training Session 43: Mutual Coverage in Defence

If we look at the training sessions in the season so far then we come to the conclusion that most exercise forms are oriented to play in the offensive. Actually every training should take the attack and the defence equally into consideration. Regrettably (but perhaps fortunately for soccer in general) defensive actions, which necessarily are part of every game, receive less attention. The combination game which we train for the building up the attack (development of automatisms) could just as well be used to develop defence. This not only applies to the defence players. A forward who loses the ball to his opponent right in front of the goal, then immediately stops and puts his hands in his pockets..., lets down his team-mates. For he should have immediately disrupted in order to help his team-mates in their defensive play. This is just one example of what we can observe week after week with all its consequences. On the attack everything is well prepared, the players offer themselves mutually and people talk about teamwork. In contrast the players in defence often have to move in when everything is practically too late. Organised defence, however, must be practised just as much as attack combinations. For this, however, you need versatile players, that is a necessity in modern soccer.

Mutual covering is an important automatism which must be applied on the whole field when the ball is lost. Helping your team-mate when he has already been eliminated is of course rather late and also difficult. But if a player knows that he

has good coverage to support him and a team-mate will come to his assistance in time, he will surely put more effort into trying to stop the opposing attack.

Now let us come to the practical situations. After a good warm-up we take another 10 minutes to prepare the players in the group.

The players run around easily, without any prescribed direction. At a signal they quickly run in the direction indicated. The coach gives the necessary instructions (many stops, run backwards often). We start at a pace which is not too high and with regular changes of direction. We not only raise the pace systematically, but also change the rhythm so that we finish with a rapid sequence of changes of direction. Jumps (point upwards) and crouches (point downwards) can also be added.

Main part

EXERCISES FOR TWO PLAYERS: DELAYING DEFENCE
One of the two players brakes the action of the person with the ball in order to give his team-mates time to get into a covering position.

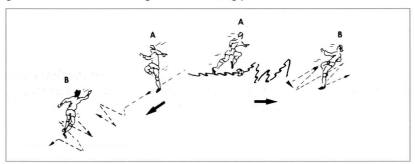

Exercise 1: Without the ball. Player A moves up while B tries to stop him while moving back. Afterwards the same with the ball.

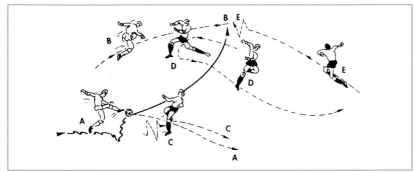

Exercise 2: Two attackers (A and B) and three defenders (C, D and E). E is the free man. As soon as defender D has been eliminated, C takes over his position and D accelerates in order to take over the role of the free man, etc.

Exercise 3: Three attackers and two defenders. Player A moves up and defender D brakes him. A passes to B. He plays to partner C, who runs past E. Free defender F comes to help. E, now out played, dashes to the free position of F and joins in if necessary.

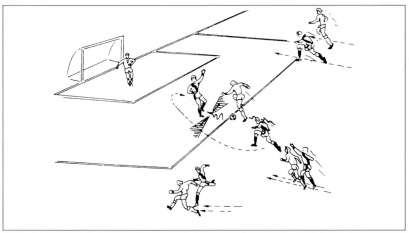

Exercise 4: Game towards a goal with covering by the free man. The attackers are only passively disrupted by the defenders. The outplayed defender hurries back and takes up the position of the partner who came to his aid. The defenders always keep a (changing) free last man. Emphasis: covering behaviour.

Training Session 44: Fitness Training with a Partner

Today's fitness training can actually be used at any time during the season. This training needs little preparation. For the exercises we do not need any materials. We get the players to alternatively carry out (strength) stretching exercises and generally developing exercises. For the (strength) stretching exercises, two players always work together; each exercise is carried out in two series of 10 repeats. For the generally developing exercises the players work against each other one after the other in 2 series of 5 repeats. Each series lasts about 1 minute, after a short break the series is repeated. The emphasis is on the generally developing exercises which should be carried out at maximum intensity. The stretching exercises serve as compensation.

 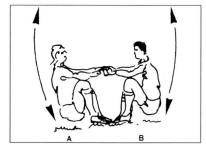

Warm-up

The players work in two waves across the width of a field. In running they mutually overtake each other. The warm-up is ended with a number of powerful dashes with changes of pace. Slow down and divide up into groups of two.

Main part

(STRENGTH) STRETCHING EXERCISES

The players crouch opposite each other. Link hands. Stand up together in one movement, sit down again and get up again. Variant: A up and B crouching down and carry on, alternating.

Exercise 1

Exercise 2

Exercise 3

Exercise 4 **B**   **A**

Exercise 5

GENERALLY DEVELOPING EXERCISES

Exercise 1: The players run behind each other, whereby the last always dashes past the first in rapid sequence. Variant: After the dash slow down, while the second man dashes to the lead with a change of pace.

Exercise 2: The players stand opposite each other bending forwards with legs straddled, hands on the upper arm or shoulder of the partner, turn the torso to left and right, spring back.

Exercise 3: The players again run behind each other. The leader constantly changes the pace and direction, whereby his partner follows as quickly as possible. Change roles every 20 metres and systematically make the exercise more difficult with numerous deceptive manoeuvres. Try to shake off the pursuer.

Exercise 4: The players again stand opposite each other with straddled legs. The partners clasp each other's right (or left) hand. Player A begins to pull B towards him (as far as possible, whereby the feet do not move). Then B pulls (as in sawing).

Exercise 5: Player A runs backwards, player B forwards. B overtakes A with a body feint. Now A runs forwards, while B in turn runs backwards, then repeat. Place the emphasis on deceptions and sudden short accelerations.

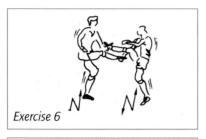

Exercise 6

Exercise 7

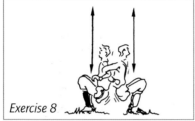

Exercise 8

Exercise 9

Exercise 10

Exercise 11

Exercise 6: The players stand facing each other again. They take their partner's right foot in their left hand: Hop on one leg (10 times), then with the other leg. Emphasis on jumping frequency or the movement itself. The players do not hop on the spot, but move around.

Exercise 7: Shadow. The players run behind each other. With a short zigzag run player A tries to disrupt his pursuers rhythm and shake him off. Change roles every 20 m.

Exercise 8: The players stand back to back. With linked arms go into a crouch and stand up again.

Exercise 9: Leapfrog. The players jump in such a way that in a single movement they jump over their partner and immediately after landing stand still ready to be jumped over. Systematically increase the pace or the jumping height.

Exercise 10: The players stand behind each other. Player A pushes player B. B provides the necessary resistance. Variant: Now player A pulls his partner.

Exercise 11: Piggyback. The players change every 20 m. Emphasis: pace and frequent changing (e.g. every 5 m).

Exercise 12

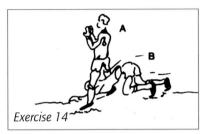

Exercise 14

Exercise 13

Exercise 15

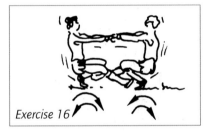

Exercise 16

Exercise 12: The players stand side by side and try to put each other off balance by barging.

Exercise 13: From a run do frog jumps. Try to jump as high as possible; cushion deeply on landing.

Exercise 14: The players stand behind each other; player A in a sidewards straddle. Player B crawls through his legs and stands in front of A.

Exercise 15: From a run do crouch jumps.

Exercise 16: Cossack dance. A very intensive exercise. The players crouch, firmly hold each other's hands, the right leg is forwards in each case, alternately jump up and stretch the right and left leg forwards (at a signal from one of the players).

Training Session 45:
Soccer Training in Station Training Situations

For the last time up we organise a training using stations. Today various game-technical exercises for three players are on the programme.

This station training has the function of letting the players train a great number of technical elements. The stations are gone through three times with the emphasis on:
- a typically clean and precise execution,
- speed of execution,
- as a complex exercise under time pressure.

Exercise 1: Two balls are needed. Hold the balls in the air and alternately pass them on to the free team-mate. Options: Only with your foot, head or either. Pay attention to clean execution and clean playing on of the ball to the free man so that he can directly march off.

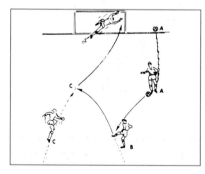

Exercise 2: With the goalkeeper. One ball is needed. Player A moves the ball from the baseline towards player B and plays to him. B immediately plays to C as C dashes in, and C shoots at the goal. Player C gets the ball and starts from position A while players A and B have meanwhile moved back one position. Optionally: Clean goal shot (instep) or play around the goalkeeper as he comes out.

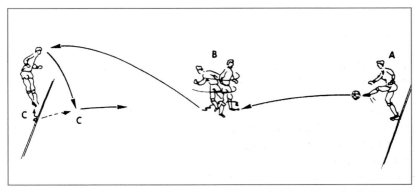

Exercise 3: One ball is needed. Player B (change regularly) receives the ball from A and plays on to C (and reverse sequence). Low and high passes.

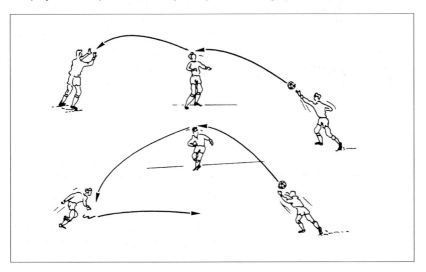

Exercise 4: Heading exercise. One ball is needed. Options: High, low, head on to a third player. Emphasis on accuracy and clean execution. When jumping to head, pay attention to clean timing.

Exercise 5: Each player has his own cone (goal) to defend. The person in possession of the ball plays against two opponents who try to get the ball. Good shielding of the ball is very important, or sudden switching from one goal to the other. Very strenuous exercise.

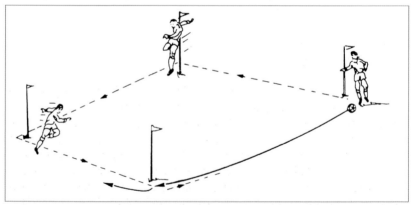

Exercise 6: One ball is needed. This is played by three players over four stations. The player closest to the ball dashes to the unoccupied position to which the ball is played. The other two sprint in the opposite direction to the pass. After a bit of practice the three players must be constantly in motion and the ball always moving.

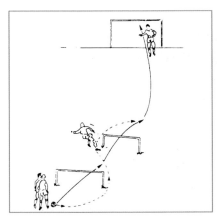

Exercise 7: Combination exercise with goal shot. This is a complex exercise with various requirements.
- Accuracy: Clean passes and precise shot
- Speed ability: Jump over the hurdles and play the pass in such a way that the goalkeeper cannot reach it
- Reaction speed and acting under time pressure: Combination of short passes and tempo play by the players so that they only just come to shoot.

Training Session 46: Getting Oriented and Offering Oneself

The attentive coach has already worked out that the annual programme must be oriented to the following points:
- Good Fitness
- Game without the ball
- Receiving and playing on the ball while moving.

Analyses show that modern soccer has greatly changed within a few years. The days of purely technical play are practically over; a midfield player carries out more than 100 dashes in a game. Whereas one used to assume that for example a defender did not have to be particularly fit, today the opposite applies. In the various systems in which everyone attacks and everyone defends, more importance is attributed to the physical qualities of every player. This is the reason we place so much importance in our programme e.g. on changes of pace and direction in the sense of "speeding up the game" and "taking the pace out of the game", but also physical involvement in defence, playing without the ball and the speed of execution of the early movement. Fortunately the latter means that technical soccer has not yet been written off. Good ball mastery is still the foundation. But the technicians must also be in good physical fitness and have the strength to fend off the direct attacks of the opponent. In order to build up sufficient fitness we carry out a load intensive training and therefore every exercise takes place against a background of movement. Standing around is a thing of the past. Every game is equally exhausting for both combatants and thus the fitter players have the advantage. In order to expose the players to these high loads in training we focus on soccer-specific movements with all their variations and avoid monotonous "lap running". At the beginning of the warm-up we get the players to work in pairs. Each pair has a ball.

Main part

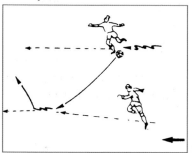

Exercise 1: Both players level with each other at a light trot:
- Moving the ball and passing it into the path of the team mate every 10 m
- Alternately with the inner and outer instep
- Pass behind the team-mate, who stops, gets the ball under control and starts again with the ball
- Play the ball to the man: let the ball just go past and then receive it with the inner instep.

Exercise 2: A number of variations of the exercise in the same formation:
- Person with the ball moves the ball, plays it forward a few metres and runs after it, controls the ball and passes it to the partner
- The same, but now after the dash directly play the ball on
- Increase and reduce the length of the passes and the running pace.

Exercise 3: The same formation. The person with the ball moves it, place the ball 5 to 7 metres forwards, dashes and stops the ball with the sole of his foot. He then plays the ball on to his partner.

Exercise 4: One player moves the ball. His partner comes towards him backwards until he is 7 m away. Pass from the person with the ball, who then dashes past his partner, turns around and runs backwards. Meanwhile the partner has the ball under control, turns with the ball, passes and in turn dashes away.

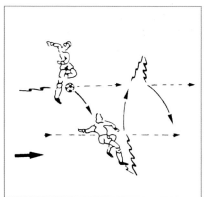

Exercise 5: The players run next to each other. The person with the ball passes, and his partner receives the ball and runs about 1 m with the ball (crossways) and then runs with the ball back to the starting position.

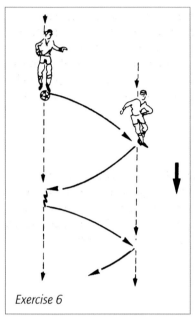

Exercise 6

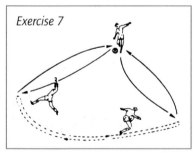

Exercise 7

Exercise 6: Technically clean wall pass play. Emphasis: speed ability and change of pace. Make sure each pass is played accurately. Variant 1: Short wall passes. Variant 2: Short first pass during the wall pass and then long return pass.

Exercise 7: The partners play the ball backwards and forwards a few times while standing still, suddenly one of the players plays about 10 m next to the partner who sprints into the pass. Afterwards backwards and forwards again while standing. Variant: The players get the partner to dash 7 to 10 times in a row.

Exercise 8: Moving the ball - Passing - Reception. Players A and B stand - both with the ball - about 15 m apart. They move their balls until they are about 2 m apart, and play the balls through short and low, turn around and sprint after their partner's pass. Go back into position and repeat.

Exercise 8

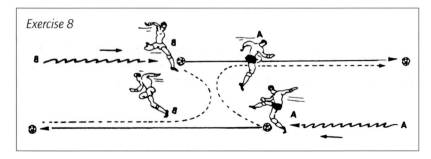

Exercise 9

Exercise 9: Three players run easily in a circle. The person with the ball passes into the path of the partner further away and dashes (together with the third player) about 10 m forwards. The player who has been passed to must run after the pass.

Exercise 10

Exercise 10: Wall pass. Two attackers, one defender. Begin slowly and make sure of accuracy (technique), then systematically increase the pace. Pay attention to the second part of the wall pass.

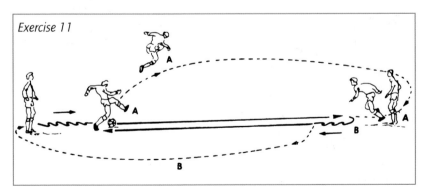

Exercise 11

Exercise 11: Pass with change of place. Two pairs about 15 m apart. Player A begins, moves the ball 5 m, makes a long pass to B (other group) and runs after the ball. Afterwards B carries out a pass with change of place.

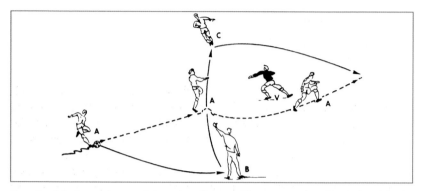

Exercise 12: Four players. Feigned wall pass. Player A moves forwards with the ball, passes to partner B and calls to get the ball back. Instead he lets the ball goes through to C and quickly brakes. Player C passes past the defender to A who suddenly dashes in.

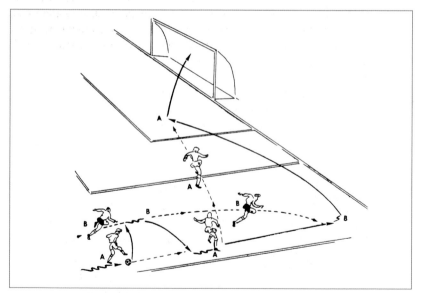

Exercise 13: Attack in pairs on the outside line. Player A moves up along the outside line. Wall pass with B. Then A passes along the outside line. Suddenly A changes his direction (towards the goal) and receives the pass into his path from B. Goal shot.

Training Session 47:
Running Training with the Ball -
Aspects Appropriate to the Game

However well a training may have been worked out, it is never an objective in itself, but always the tool, e.g. to build up fitness or to improve playing. Thus a coach will regularly direct his attention to collective tactics and the system he has chosen for his team. It is important that in doing so he does not sacrifice the individual qualities of the players to the game system too much in order to avoid a stereotype game which hardly provides any surprises. The trick is therefore to develop a system which takes the individual possibilities of the team into consideration. How do we arrive at the necessary subjects for the various training sessions? The answer is simple. Because the training objective is the optimum preparation of the game, training is best built up on game situations. It is not difficult for an attentive coach to put together exercise objectives from the game moves of a points game. Such moves with their varying stations, however, are too complex to function as an exercise altogether. Therefore we will first examine which principles are made clear by these moves, for example: correct passing on of the ball or coordination of play without the ball. Exercises based on this have the following objectives:
- Improvement of peripheral vision
- Development of a feeling for where a team mate his
- Correct timing on taking up positions
- Correct playing of the ball followed by a support by a team mates.

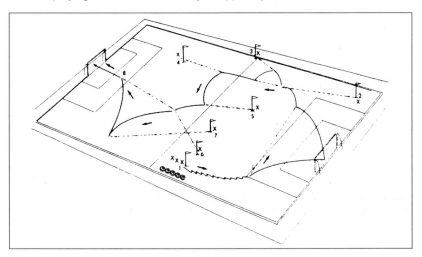

In other words: We break the whole chain of action down into individual elements (analysis) so that each element corresponds to an individual action. We then join these elements together in an exercise (synthesis). Here is an example of this. First let us divide the game situation into various stations (cf. the numbers in the diagram):

1. In a defensive action we intercept a centre pass and thus gain ball possession. In order to get relief the player moves the ball on towards his own goal, plays back to the goalkeeper who shifts the game to the other side.

2. The outer defender moves up and gains the ball.

3. A midfield player ties up his opponent and plays a wall pass with the outer defender who then moves up again.

4. A midfield player helps and gets the ball from the outer defender.

5. A second midfield player moves up with him and receives a cross pass close to the centre circle.

6. On the other outside line a midfield player dashes and receives the ball passed to him directly.

7. From the centre a player offers himself on the outside line and is played to with a pass upfield.

8. This player plays the ball on: a team-mate has run on without stopping and shoots at the goal. In this game situation you thus find a series of simple game moves. Today's training will be based on this.

Warm-up

The warm-up will gradually merge into the main part of the training. Have we begin easily and slowly increase the demands. The players divide up into groups of eight. The groups work separately and divide themselves into two groups of three and one group of two, formation as in the diagram. The players in Group 1

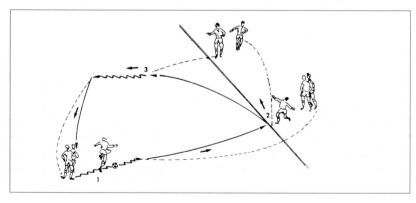

have 2 balls. Begin easily. After making a pass go in an arc around the outside and close up to Group 2 again so that the execution of the exercise is not disrupted. A player from Group 1 moves the ball towards Group 2, passes and closes up behind this group. The player from Group 2 who receives the ball plays it directly 10 m in front of Group 3. A player from that group runs in, gets the ball under control, dribbles and plays it back to Group 1. This player then closes up to Group 1. The moment the first player from Group 2 plays the ball on, the second player in Group 1 begins with the exercise. Gradually increase the pace until the closing up is done in a sprint.

Main part

Thus with the warm-up already we have introduced the actual training. As we on we add up one more station each time and always begin with Station 1. Every exercise is carried out continuously until all players have had a turn. When the exercise is over the players take up position for the next exercise which is then extended by one position. In this regard, look at the overview sketch at the beginning of the training session.

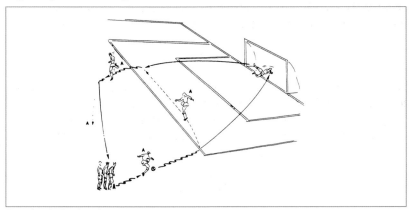

Exercise 1: Station 1.
The players start from position 1. They move the ball as far as the penalty area, play towards the goalkeeper and sprint to the other side of the penalty area. The goalkeeper throws the ball to the other side (shifting the game), ball reception, move up a few metres with the ball at your foot and then play back to the starting position. Then close up to Group A in a sprint. Increase the pace and regularly change the goalkeeper. When the whole thing is moving quickly, Station 2 is added. For this a player positions himself at point B (see the following diagram).

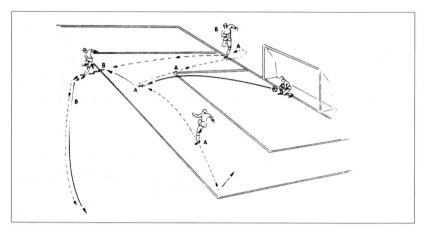

Exercise 2: Stations 1 and 2.
We add Station e the previous Exercise. The moment we receive the ball, the player at position B starts. We play the ball into his path and close up ourselves at position B. Player B moves the ball a few metres at his foot, then plays it back to the starting point where he also closes up. Emphasis: timing and running in from position B.

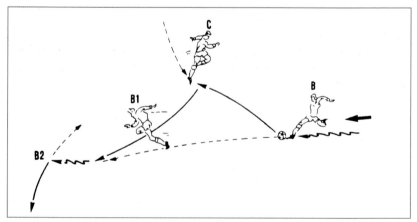

Exercise 3: Stations 1 to 3.
We add another element to the exercise: an outer defender B plays a wall pass with midfield player C who comes in to help. After the wall pass is finished, B plays the ball back to the starting position A and himself moves to position C, while C - after passing back the ball in the wall pass - sprints to close up at starting position A of Station 1.

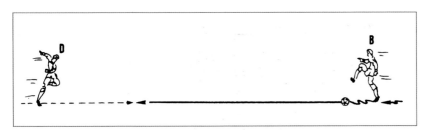

Exercise 4: Stations 1 to 4
After a wall pass B plays the ball on to player D as he comes back. B then takes up position C and D plays the ball back to starting position A where he closes up. After the wall pass with player B, player C takes up position D.

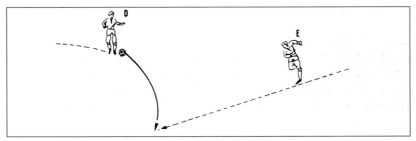

Exercise 5: Stations 1 to 5.
The midfield player D, coming back, puts the ball into the path of E as he dashes in, who plays the ball back to the starting position A. E sprints to position A, and D takes over E's position.

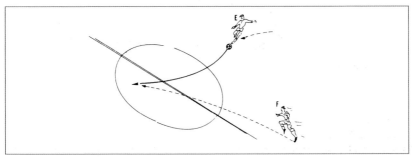

Exercise 6: Stations 1 to 6.
A further extension of the exercise. Player E gets the ball passed to him under control and passes it into the path of F as he dashes in (centre circle). F plays the ball back to starting position A and then closes up there. E takes up the position of F etc.

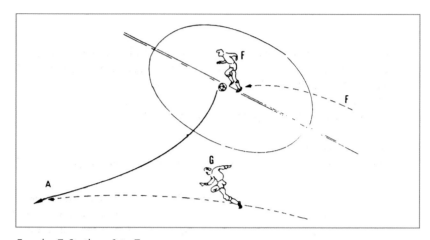

Exercise 7: Stations 1 to 7 .
Player F sprints forwards (centre circle) and passes to player G who dashes to the outside line. G plays back to starting position A, F takes up the position of G.

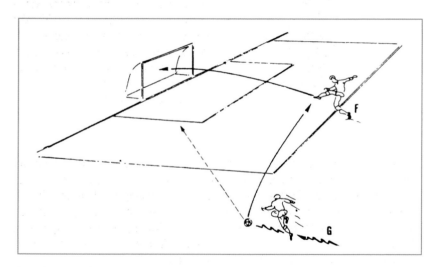

Exercise 8: Stations 1 to 8.
Complete execution of the attack move. From the outside line player G lays the ball on for player F who has sprinted up from the centre circle.

Training Session 48: The Lob

The lob can be employed both from a standing position and from a playing movement. From a standing position: in particular in the case of (direct) free kicks close to the goal in order to get the ball over the wall.
While moving:
- Shifting the game in the final phase of an attack
- Pass in front of the goal
- Eliminating a defender coming out
- In particular when shooting at the goal, when the goalkeeper comes out.

The lob is one of the techniques which is relatively difficult to learn because it is mostly a matter of centimetres and is carried out under constantly changing and often difficult circumstances. In today's training we will cover the use of the lob when attacking. After the warm-up we immediately begin with the technical part of the training. Because the training is oriented to the game we will keep the technique training short so that we have more time to apply the technique and the tactic.

Main part

Begin first with a demonstration and a corresponding explanation of the long and short lob. Long: Eyes on the ball, standing leg 15 to 20 cm next to the ball. At the last moment lean your body slightly backwards. Leg swings out from the hip in a circular movement. Hit the ball in the lower half, involving your big toe. Stretch your standing leg from the heel upwards (roll off). Swing your kicking leg after at the ball in a follow-through. Short: "Peck" the ball more. The movement comes more from the knee, while the shooting leg brakes.

TRAINING TECHNIQUE

Exercise 1:
The players stand opposite each other about 10 m apart. Execution of the lob:
a) Play into the hands of the partner
b) Controlled by the partner and return pass c) Reduce and increase the distance have.

Exercise 2:
The same exercise, but lob the ball over the partner who then turns and in running receives the ball. The first player goes along and now the second player plays a lob.

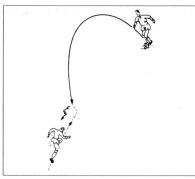

Exercise 3:
In this exercise the player who will receive the ball is constantly moving:
a) He increases and reduces the distance to the person with the ball.
b) He "breaks out" to the left and right. In the first part the initiative lies with the person with the ball. He calls or points to where he will play the lob and the team-mate reacts accordingly. Then the initiative is with the player receiving the ball. He calls for the ball to be played in a certain direction, possibly with a feinting movement: e.g. calls for the ball to the left and first pretends to sprint to the right.

Exercise 1

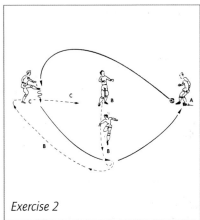

Exercise 2

GAME-LIKE EXERCISES

Exercise 1: Three players, 1 ball. Player A moves the ball towards B and passes this to him close to the ground. Player B clears with a lob. Now A takes up the position of B, while B tries to prevent the pass from C to A by moving up.

Exercise 2: Three players, 1 ball. Player A begins by lobbing the ball over B to C. Player C plays the ball directly into the path of D who calls for the ball while moving and plays it on to A. Now C moves up to position B, while B takes over the position of C.

Exercise 3

Exercise 3: Three players and goalkeeper: lob towards the goal. Player A, in ball possession, lobs the ball over T (e.g. coach) to B, who diverts the ball towards A, who is moving up. He then brings the ball under control and drives it in the direction of the goal where the goalkeeper runs towards it. Now A tries to overcome the goalkeeper with a lob and thus to score a goal.

Exercise 4: Elimination of a defender. In this exercise player A must make good a mistake of his partner B. Player B moves up with the ball at his feet and stands in front of defender V. He therefore plays back to team mate A, whereupon defender V attacks the new person with the ball, A. B at first stands still and tries to get the ball back from A to a free position, dashes upfield, whereupon A chooses the best way and overcomes V with a lob - in the direction of B as he moves up.

GAME-TACTICAL EXERCISES

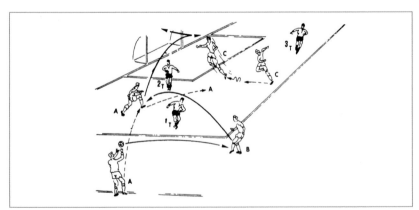

Exercise 1: A throws the ball towards B. He lobs the ball to A as the latter runs in, who then lays the ball on in turn with a lob so that C, who has pushed forward, can do a header towards the goal. At first practise it calmly. Then add a passive defender. Afterwards at normal game pace with a third defender who tries to hinder C from heading at the goal. When the defenders are added, at the same time integrate the goalkeeper into the exercise.

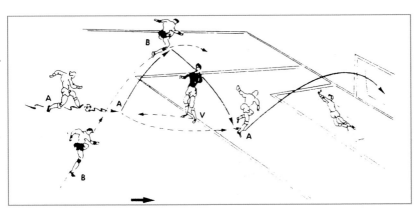

Exercise 2: Three players and goalkeeper. Attack and outplaying of the goalkeeper. Player A, in ball possession, moves up towards V, while team-mate B runs freely behind him diagonally. Play a wall pass, whereby the goalkeeper leaves the goal in order to shorten the angle. The goalkeeper goes out far enough that A can try to score a goal with a lob. Again, first practise clean technique, then increase the pace.

TRAINING GAME 8 AGAINST 8

Exercises are important, but we must not forget the training games in which the exercises are put into practice and the playing creativity of the players is challenged. We do, however, provide rules and set an objective which we want to achieve. Today we want to play a game of 8 against 8 across the whole field so that the players experience the space and how this can be used offensively and must be used defensively.

Training Session 49:
Fitness Training in Station Training Situations

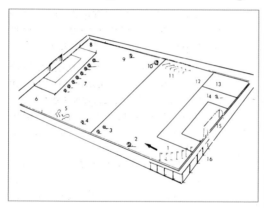

Today we carry out a fitness training using station which the players carry out in pairs, station for station. The objective is to improve running with changes of pace. At the same time assertiveness with the ball is addressed. The illustration shows which aids we need and how these are set up on the field. We need: 14 balls, 2 ropes, 7 flagpoles or cones, 6 hurdles and 2 medicine balls. Organisation: 80 seconds practising per station, 15 seconds break for moving on to the next station. As soon as station 16 has been reached, run around the field once easily and start again. Three rounds.

Warm-up

Let the players take the initiative themselves in small groups. The player running at the front demonstrates the exercise which is copied by the other players. Regularly swap the positions. The coach only gives comments and tips now and then, in order to increase the load during the warm-up with a view to the main part.

Main part

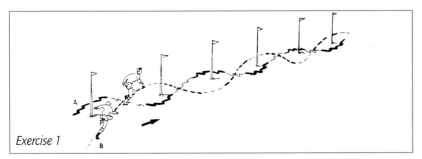

Exercise 1

Exercise 1: Flagpoles. The players run alone or in pairs (close together) between the flagpoles, around each one or along the row of poles. Also accelerations, whereby the changes of pace (slow down the pace) must not be forgotten.

Exercise 2

Exercise 3

Exercise 2: Medicine ball exercise. Both players throw each other the ball in various ways. If the players are close to each other - increase the speed; if they are further apart - increase the use of strength.

Right from the start the coach makes sure that all necessary equipment is left for the next group after the exercise has been finished. The coach goes from one station to the other and ensures that everywhere players are practising intensively.

Exercise 3: "Conjure" easily with the ball. Keep the ball in the air as long as possible, freely and with your head (count along).

Exercise 4

Exercise 5

Exercise 4: Man against man. The person with the ball tries to keep the opponent away from the ball by shielding it and then suddenly creating space with a short acceleration and going back into position. There is most room for such running work in the centre of the pitch. Shake off the opponent with repeated changes of pace.

Exercise 5: Skipping: Closing hops, one legged jumps etc.

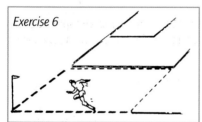

Exercise 6

Exercise 6: Sprinting. In the corner sprint along the lines. Sprint along two lengths, then easily run two lengths.

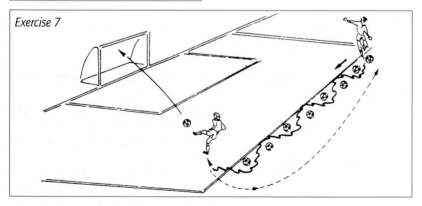

Exercise 7

Exercise 7: Take the first ball along, slalom around the balls and shoot at goal. Get the ball again and put it back in its place.

Exercise 8

Exercise 8: Carrying. Piggyback, on your arms etc. The first time the players carry their partner for a longer period, later quickly change carriers.

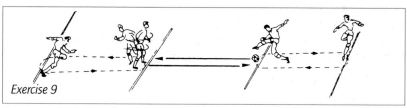

Exercise 9

Exercise 9: Accordion. Accelerate and play the ball, turn around and sprint back to the starting point. Pay attention to timing so that the ball is played back and forth in a flowing manner.

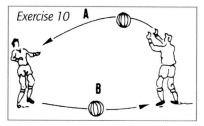

Exercise 10   **A**   **B**

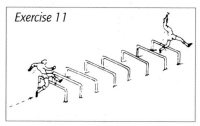

Exercise 11

Exercise 10: Medicine ball throwing. At a fast pace player A always throws the ball high and player B throws it back low. After 10 throws each, change.

Exercise 12

Exercise 11: Hurdles. Jumps and sprints over and around the hurdles. Emphasis on smoothness of the jumps, afterwards on speed.

Exercise 12: Leapfrog. A short run-up, but at high speed. Jump - and on landing immediately get in position to be jumped over. Alternately emphasise jumping distance or height.

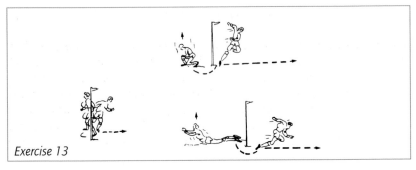

Exercise 13

Exercise 13: Acceleration from various starting positions as a competition between partners.

Exercise 14

Exercise 14: Heading while jumping-with or without a run up-at a predetermined point.

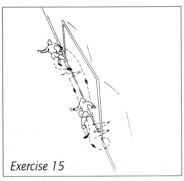

Exercise 15

Exercise 15: Inclusion of the goal posts. Accelerations with short and fast body feints in front of the post with a short turn around the post and back.

Exercise 16

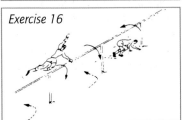

Exercise 16: Railing. Between two posts, Jump over the railing, then crawl back under the railing. Then practise for one minute at the highest pace possible.

Training _   Free Spaces

A player would p   ‍ ‍ ‍ ‍ ‍ ‍ ‍ ‍ der ideal conditions. Not only the kind
of pass plays a rc   tion in which he receives the ball,
namely whether or nc   who tries to get the ball off him or
make it more difficult tc   we can get around these risks e.g.
by directly playing the ban   ayed at a high pace the opponent
of course has little chance   nother way of cutting out the
opponent is to create space h   to receive the ball. We can
create the space in the following \

- Use the neglected zone: A game takes such a course that we do not use a certain area in the opponents' goal zone, e.g. the left or the right wing. If we do not occupy this zone then we can be fairly certain that the opponent will not sacrifice any players to cover the area we have neglected. This creates for us the possibility of bringing a midfield player or a defender into the game in this open zone during an attack.

- Create free space yourself: With a systematic way of playing we can create a free space where we can play to a team-mate. This zone is already occupied, but now our player draws his opposing player with him, so that a free area arises which we can quickly use for our attack.
  Both forms go back to the emphasis which we have tried to make clear in our annual programme:
  - Playing without the ball
  - Change of pace
  - Involving team-mates in the game.

In the game it often happens that the person with the ball sees no possibility of playing the ball away. There is no man who can be played to or a free area so that the player gets out of rhythm, raises his arms and gets stuck. In such a case the team-mates must create free space by enticing the opponent out. The player who tears the hole will not get the ball, but he creates a chance for a team-mate. Running without having the ball passed to one is often felt to be a nuisance. This is incorrect. After all, the point is that a team-mate can carry on the attack thanks to the operation and the runner. An attack in which the runner has as much of a share as the person with the ball.

Warm-up

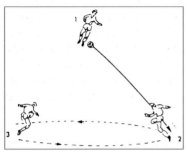

In groups of three the players loosely play the ball to each other, every now and then the ball is thrown. This is followed by a pass with change of position:
Player 1 plays to position 2 while players 2 and 3 swap places. Player 3 receives the ball. Now the ball is played from position 2 to 3 while players 1 and 2 swap places. The same with throws. Increase the pace.

Main part

The exercises are based on the following principle: The player moved up without the ball is watched over by the opponent. If the game moves in his direction, he runs (not too quickly) in the direction of events and draws his opponent with him (ties him). To hide his real intentions, he calls for the ball. A team-mate is then played to in the area which he has just freed up.

Exercise 1: Although we initially have the exercise carried out under a technical aspect, we immediately involve a defender in this first exercise in order to increase closeness to the real game situation. Player A moves up with the ball at his feet, team-mate B - guarded by a defender - runs towards A and calls for the ball. A sees that player C sprints into the area left open by B, and places the ball there. Gradually put the accent on accuracy. Not only gradually increase the pace, but also hide the real intention (acceleration by C, pass by A).

Exercise 2: Five players. After this basic exercise we practise a few practical applications. The pass along the outside line: A runs forwards along the outside line and then moves the ball right across to a defender. At this moment player C accelerates, draws his opponent with him, so that B can sprint into the free area and receive a pass from Player A. First let the players practise without opposing players and then add an opponent.

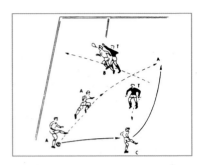

Exercise 3: Five players. Here we play to a player across the centre while the defender is also drawn outwards. Player A passes towards C. At this moment player B draws his opponent outwards with him, and player C plays to his partner A. The cross pass from A to C is necessary because A is confronted by an opponent as soon as the exercise runs quickly and smoothly.

Exercise 4: Four players. Attack on the left. Player A moves the ball towards the centre. Team-mate B creates space for C. Player C can now continue the game by optionally passing to A or B. Afterwards add a defender.

Exercise 5: Midfield game. Six players. Player A moves up forwards, player D draws the opponent towards A with him while B intercepts the running direction, runs towards the second opposing players and calls for the ball. Meanwhile C dashes into the free area behind D to which A can pass the ball on. If in the freely moving game the defender has not gone along, the player coming back (here D) is automatically free and can be played to.

It would be too simple if we could apply all the moves we have practised in games. The coach and the players therefore try to find variations of the exercises or other solutions. For Exercise 6 we need player B in order to have more certainty that the defender of D does not go along to the outside, to where the ball is first played.

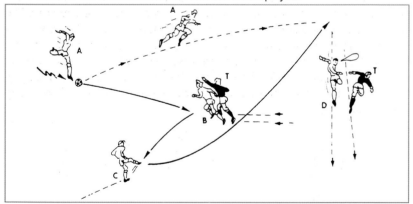

Exercise 6: Six players. Player A, in ball possession, moves up. His team-mate B calls for the ball and draws his defender with him. Now B - in contrast to the last exercise - is drawn into the game after all. He diverts the pass from A to C. Meanwhile D starts and draws his opponent with him by calling for the ball. C now plays to A as he sprints up, who then uses the free area created by D. If D's defender does not go with him, then C plays to D .

Training Session 51: Pressure Training in Groups of Four

The end of the season is in sight and how we continue training depends on our position in the league. Are we still playing at the top or must we fight relegation? In both cases motivation plays a very great role, and for the younger, less experienced players in particular it is a matter of all or nothing. In order to effectively shape the last part of the annual programme we have chosen a number of focal points which have proven to be very important in contacts with coaches. It goes without saying that these training sessions can be carried out during the whole season. Of the many possible subjects we have selected the following:
- Training under load up with the ball
- Shielding and its use
- Fitness training in game form
- The return pass
- and the most important: The goal shot.
Today we will deal with training under pressure, for four players with the ball. Of course the emphasis is on the pace in the sense of a fitness training suitable for soccer. Feeling for the ball and understanding teamwork are also not forgotten in this difficult training. After a very intensive warm-up we begin with the exercises. Put simply, these exercises are employed in between as a load exercise. The players practise for one or two minutes with all their strength. If you want to organise a short, very hard training, then you can carry out several exercises in a row with the necessary resting breaks and pulse checks, whereby the exercises are in such an order that you first have an exercise where all four players work (e.g. Exercise 1), followed by an exercise in which two players have a short resting break (Exercise 2).

Exercise 1: Heading ball and running game. Players stand in pairs about 15 m apart. Each pair has a ball. At a signal one of the two players in each case throws the ball up high, the second jumps to head it.
Both players then dash - with the ball - to the other side in each case and the ball changes players. Continuously, duration: 1 minute.

Exercise 2: Game with hurdles. Here two players are active each time, while the other two have a short resting break. As soon as the first player has turned at the flagpole, the next one starts etc. Practise continuously for three minutes.
Execution: Pass under the hurdles (1), slalom around the hurdles (or jump over them) (2), get the ball under control (3), pass again (4) and sprint to the flagpole (5), turn (6), pass to the starting position (7), slalom around the cones (8), get the ball under control (9) and pass to the partner. Close up behind.

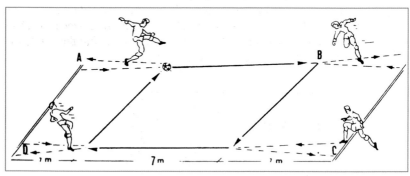

Exercise 3: Pass the ball, in doing so sprint forwards and back. Four players position themselves around a 7 m x 7 m square, each of them also 7 m from the particular corner. Player A sprints to the ball, plays to B and runs backwards to the starting point again. Player B runs into the ball, plays to C and also runs back backwards. C starts etc. 2 minutes duration.

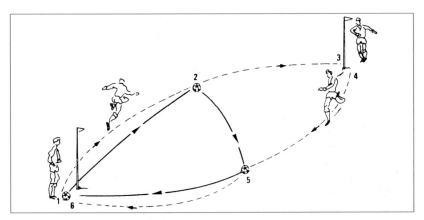

Exercise 4: Passing and sprinting on. Two players stand opposite each other at flagpoles 25 m apart. Player A passes the ball into the centre, dashes after the ball, passes to the side and sprints on to the other flagpole. Meanwhile, the other player has dashed from there to the ball, passes and dashes after the ball to the flagpole. There a new player starts. 3 minutes duration.

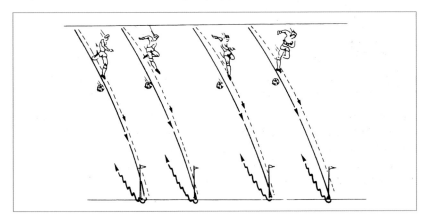

Exercise 5: Follow the ball. This is a purely sprinting exercise in which the players additionally pay attention to their use of strength when kicking the pass. At a signal pass towards the turning-point over about 15 m, sprint after the ball, at the flagpole turn, lay the ball on again, dash etc. Variant: At the turning point take the ball in hand and sprint back to the starting point.

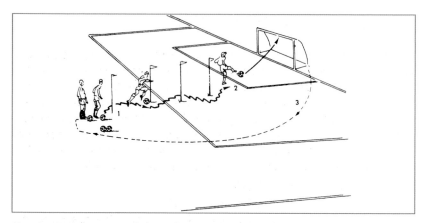

Exercise 6: Slalom around the poles and shot at the goal. The four players - each with a ball - stand behind the 4 flagpoles. The first player starts, dribbles in slalom around the poles and shoots at the goal. Then he gets the ball back and in a wide arc joins up at the back again. When the first player has started to shoot, the second starts etc. 5 minutes duration.

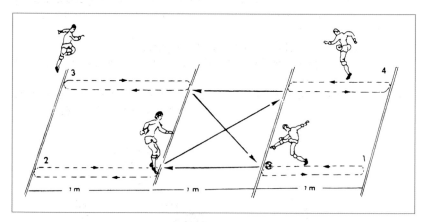

Exercise 7: Accordion game. The players form up as in exercise 3. Now, however, they pass the ball to each other, alternately with passes upfield or diagonally. Run towards the ball, then return to the starting point. The players completely expend themselves in this game. Duration: two minutes.

Training Session 52: Shielding the Ball

Although the term seems to point to a more defensive function, shielding is a purely offensive element. Even more, it is actually an element which is designed to get an attack which has got stuck back into momentum. With shielding - a kind of dribbling in pairs - you can get around this problem. One player leaves the ball standing for a team-mate while trying to shield the ball from the opposing player with his body. You have to make sure that the handover is as simple as possible. This means leaving the ball standing at the right moment and not giving it a last scoop. As an example we choose a practical game phase (Exercise 7).

Analysis of the total sequence (Exercise 7):
1. Player A moves the ball across the width of the field.
2. He is covered by an opponent (position always between the person with the ball and one's own goal).
3. A leaves the ball standing, while shielding it, however.
4. Team-mate B comes to his aid.
5. Player B takes over the ball.
6. With the ball at his foot, player B increases the pace and changes the running direction while A draws the opposing player on with him. What do we achieve with this relatively simple measure?
- With a sudden change of pace we can shift the game.
- Through the change of position of the defender we put the defence system of the opponent off balance.
- We have the opportunity to further build up our attack by bringing a team-mate into the game or shooting at the goal ourselves (see exercises 8 and 9).

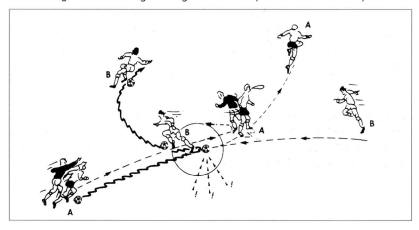

Because the sequence of movements is too complex to be able to just learn it in one go, we have broken it down into six individual elements. Each of the six elements is the core of an exercise. This has the advantage that all players understand the various movement elements and can execute them in the further course of training in the total movement with commitment and without weaknesses.

Exercise 1

Exercise 2

Exercise 3

Exercise 1: Players move the ball (at their foot) across the width of the playing field.

Exercise 2: The same exercise, but now with an opposing player on one side, therefore shield the ball.

Exercise 3: Shield the ball from the opponent, suddenly leave it standing, while you carry on running yourself.

Exercise 4

A   B

Exercise 4: Two players stand opposite each other about 25 m apart, A moves the ball towards player B who intersects the running path of player A very tightly (don't take the ball with you yet) and in doing so changes pace.

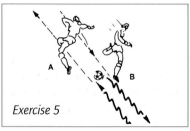

Exercise 5

Exercise 5: The same exercise, but now B takes over the ball. Player A leaves the ball standing for B. Player B takes it over and at first maintains his running direction, then accelerates and at the same time changes direction. First train exact execution, only then increase the pace.

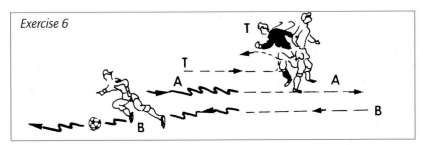

Exercise 6

Exercise 6: After that we repeat Exercise 5, adding an opposing player who directs his play to A (covering between player and goal).

After these individual elements have been practised, we join them together to make our example exercise (Exercise 7), which we can now execute game-tactically.

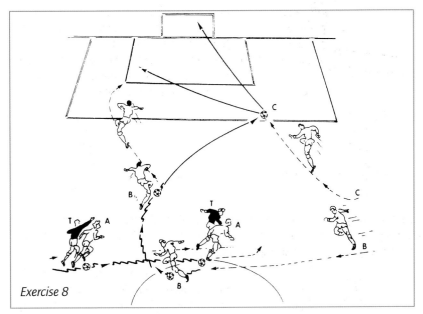

Exercise 8

Exercise 8: Player A - covered by the opponent - moves the ball across the width of the field towards team-mate B. He takes over the ball and moves up with the ball at his foot, team-mate C dashes upfield where he receives a pass from B. Player C shoots at the goal or lays the ball on in for player B as he comes in to support.

Exercise 9: Shot at goal. Get the players to carry out the shielding closer to the goal once too. After B has taken over the ball, he shoots - using coverage by A - as quickly as possible at the goal.

Exercise 10: "Fake" shielding. Also practise a situation in which B cannot take over the ball because of mutual covering or because the defender marking A orientates himself to B. In this case A runs on with the ball into the opponents' area because he is no longer man-marked, and passes. "Fake" shielding can also be used as a deceptive action.

Training Session 53:
Fitness Training in Game Form for Groups of Three

A load training must not become monotonous. Variety and a certain independence of the players increase their enthusiasm and their interest in the fitness elements of the annual programme. It should be particularly ensured that the exercises do not degenerate into monotonous running around with occasional sprints. Such a training will only be "put up with" by the players. It is better to offer a diverse programme with sprints, stops and changes of pace which the players really experience. If we add playful elements to these exercises they are certainly a tool with which to achieve our objective. In the following a number of exercise examples are given which demonstrate increasing degrees of difficulty with varying contents. Using the ball in load exercises promotes the involvement required of the players.

Organisation: The players divide up into groups of three which are maintained during the whole training session. We need one ball per group. The emphasis is on pace and timing.

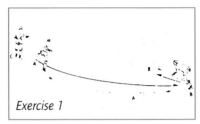

Exercise 1

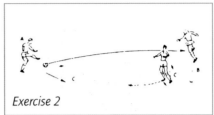

Exercise 2

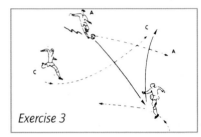

Exercise 3

Exercise 1: Keep the ball moving. Two players stand 15 m from a team-mate. Player A - in ball possession - plays the ball to partner B and runs - in a slight arc - after the pass to take up the position of B. Meanwhile player B has passed the ball back to C whereby he also sprints after the pass etc. Continuously, each player runs 10 times, followed by a resting break.

Exercise 2: "Pass to me". The players stay in the same formation as in the previous exercise. Player A tries to pass to his team-mate B but is hindered by defender C. The initiative comes from player B who, with movements (running free) and deception (pretended movement and calling for the ball on the other side) gives A the opportunity to play the ball on. Defender C - with his back to B - tries to get the passes. Continuously, regularly change roles, whereby all players play as defender 7 times.

Exercise 3: Direct passing of the ball. Here three players move around at changing paces, but in such a way that they can be played to. The emphasis lies on direct passing of the ball which makes the speed of execution very high. Players must be prepared to run after every ball and play every ball on.

Exercise 4: Two against one on a line. Two players stand opposite each other about 15 m apart. The third stands between them as defender. The content of this exercise is simple and occurs untold times in every game: Eliminate an opposing player with brief shifting of the game and a skilful pass. Make sure the players do not run across the width. Deception and passing are the weapons. The defender may use any tactics he wants to, e.g. running towards the players or provoking a bad pass with pretended movements. Have the game carried out very intensively.

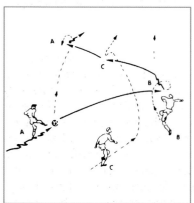

Exercise 5: Intensification - three players, pass behind. Three players stand next to each other across a wide front. The game goes across the width of the field. Players combine and move up in doing so, constantly passing the ball. The pass, however, must always be played just behind the man. To do this the player with the ball does a brief sprint, stops, turns and receives the ball. Players make sure they can always be played to. Gradually increase the pace.

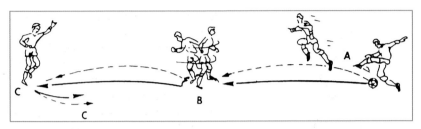

Exercise 6: Keep moving. The players stand on a line, about 8 m apart. Player A - in ball possession - passes to B and sprints after his pass in the direction of position B. Meanwhile player B receives the ball, carries out a half turn with the ball and passes to C, also following his pass. Player C now passes to A who in the meantime is standing ready etc. Continuous.

Exercise 7: Support in running backwards. Three players stand facing each other at three corners of an equilateral triangle. The distance between the players is 8 m. In the exercise A and B move forwards, while C runs backwards. Player A passes to C who passes back to B. He again plays to C etc.

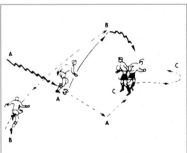

Exercise 8: Cross combination with a half active defender. Initial formation as in Exercise 7. Now, however, constantly change their positions while C brakes as far as possible and then gets into position in time. Player A moves the ball towards defender C who prevents him going through alone by stopping him. Meanwhile team-mate B runs through behind A and receives a pass from A in the free area. Player A dashes diagonally on without the ball in order to get into position for the next pass, while C gets into position with a sprint. Now player B starts. Do not simply have the exercise run at the same pace, but set very clear accents: Game with the ball by A in the direction of the defender (I want to get past), sudden support (change of pace) by B and energetic pushing back by C (short, powerful sprints).

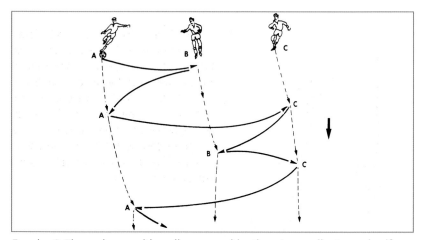

Exercise 9: Three players with wall pass combination. An excellent exercise if you are able to use it fully. The players develop their game in a wide front across the length of the field (the groups start 20 m apart). Each time a wall pass is played, followed by a through pass with player B as the position to be passed to.

Never run at a constant pace, but vary the exercise with changes of pace (wall pass), stopping, cross and dashing in. Also put in a defender who "offers himself", provokes a wall pass and then lets himself be fooled by a lob across the width.

Training Session 54: Return Pass

Often a difficult attack or defence situation can be solved by shifting the game with a return pass. In the last phase of attack for example, balls are often kicked randomly in front of the goal, usually with relatively little success. If, however, you move the ball back in such a situation, you can turn a defence upside down. A pass to the rear, in other words before the defence moving back, to a team-mate moving up, makes this possible for a brief moment. It goes without saying that precision and timing play a great role here.

Main part

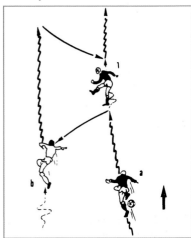

Exercise 1: In pairs with one ball. Players begin level with each other. Player A, who has the ball, increases the pace, while B stops. A then puts the ball back for B who sprints to the ball. Now B must raise the pace and put the ball back for A etc. Systematically pay more attention to the change of pace with the ball and ensure accurate playing back of the ball into the path of your team-mate.

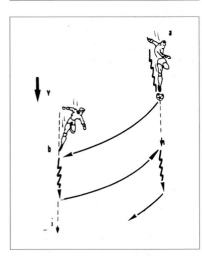

Exercise 2: The same formation. Now player B calls for the ball by changing pace. Player A passes the ball into the path of B who sends it back for A. He then receives the ball again and changes the pace, whereupon player B starts again and calls for the ball. Continuous.

Exercise 3: Player B stands 5 to 7 m in front of A. The players run into the depth of the field, with A regularly playing the ball on to B, who then directly plays it back. Systematically increase the pace.

PREPARATORY GAME-TACTICAL EXERCISES

For the next exercise we place 3 flagpoles in the goal area. We practise without defenders, for these have a disruptive effect here: Because they know that the ball will be moved back, they can be prepared and get the ball back with certainty.

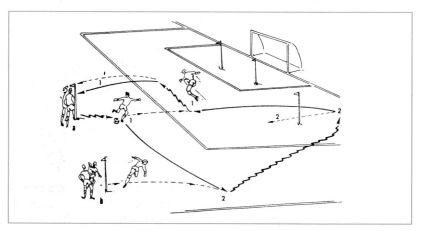

Exercise 1: The first player from Group A moves up - with the ball at his foot - and passes to the starting player of Group B. This person moves the ball to the baseline and puts it back to player A who receives the ball, turns away and plays back to his group where he closes up again. Player B also closes up to his group across the outside line. The emphasis is on sprints, moving the ball, the accuracy of the pass and timing.

Exercise 2: Player A passes the ball to player B who puts the ball back for player A. The latter now places the ball behind player B who runs into the pass, moves the ball to the side and plays it back for the group which he closes up to in an arc. Meanwhile player A has taken over the position of player B.

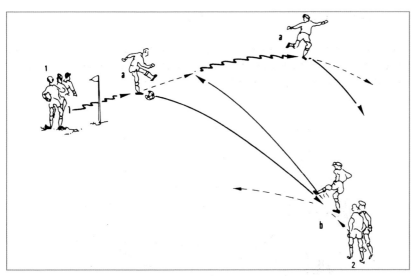

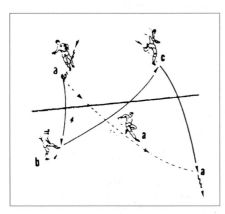

Exercise 3: Player A - the ball at his foot - moves up and passes across to team-mate B coming in to support him. The latter plays the ball back hard into the path, A goes to the ball and changes his pace while doing so. He then plays the ball back to Group B which he then joins while player B has run to Group A. Thanks to this role change every player can play in every position.

GAME-TACTICAL EXERCISES

Exercise 1: Return pass in the mid-field. Player A moves up. Team-mate B offers himself and receives the ball from A. Now player B sends the ball back diagonally to C who passes to player A as he sprints through into the depth of the field. Player B takes over the place of A.

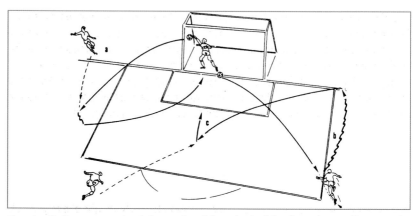

Exercise 2: Return pass in defence. By giving the ball back to the goalkeeper who can then throw this to the other side, an initial disruptive action of the opponent can be escaped from. The goalkeeper throws to outer defender A who takes the ball with him, but then suddenly turns and plays back to his goalkeeper. The latter throws the ball to the other side to team-mate B who has run into position. To complete this training exercise, we get this player to move the ball as far as the goal area line and move it back for a third player who dashes in and shoots at the goal.

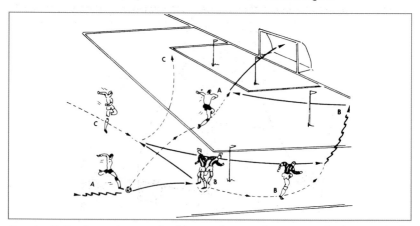

Exercise 3: Total attack move. In this attack move the opportunity is created - by putting the ball back - to pass to a midfield player in the zone which has been left free, who in turn plays the ball back in order to create a chance of scoring a goal. Execution: Initially without opposing players, instead we take a flagpole. Player A moves up on the outside line and passes to partner B (is covered behind), who

directly plays back to C. The latter plays the ball into the area into which B runs. Player B now moves the ball to the goal area line and places it in front of the returning defenders (flagpoles), player A, who has run through , then shoots at the goal. Variant: Player B shoots the ball between the defenders or lobs it over them. Finally we include a defender in the exercise. Putting the ball back or kicking a return pass is thus not a solution for embarrassing situations as long as it does not become routine, but rather a sensible preparation for closing the attack.

Training Session 55: Goal Shot

In this penultimate example we turn our attention to the highlight of every attack: the goal shot. It goes without saying that it is not our intention to place this training at the end of an exercise series. The goal shot must be trained right from the start as part of the attack. Really we can close all the attack exercises we have discussed so far with a shot at goal.

Exercise 1: A player moves the ball and while running shoots at the goal.

Exercise 2: A player lays the ball on a few metres and immediately shoots at the goal.

Exercise 3: A player runs into a diagonal pass and immediately shoots at the goal.

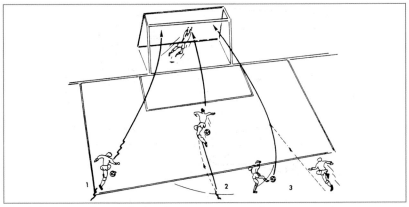

All of these exercises and also the next one are of course not always executed from the same starting position. If the game moves are practised at all possible positions, then the players naturally develop a variable ball and goal shot feeling. In the following combination exercises we include a team-mate. The goal scorer hides his intentions.

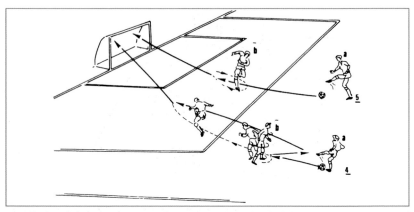

Exercise 4: Player A passes to player B. He lets the ball bounce back, turns and receives the pass from A in a sprint.

Exercise 5: Player B runs towards player A who places the ball behind B. Player B pretends to receive the ball, but lets it goes past, turns and shoots at the goal.

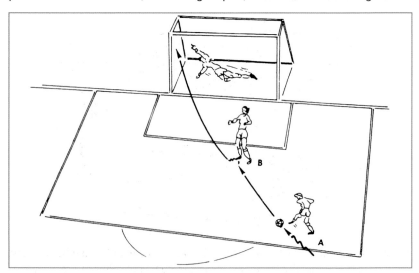

Exercise 6: Goal shot from a turn. The player who will shoot at goal receives the ball, whereby he stands with his back to the goal. Receive the ball, turn and, possibly with a feint, shoot at goal.

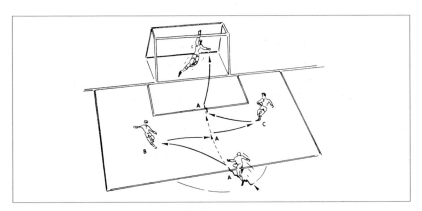

Exercise 7: Wall pass with goal shot. In view of the fact that a wall pass is regularly used in the game in preparation for a goal shot, we cannot practise its clean execution often enough. A wall pass followed by a goal shot creates an exercise which is very close to the game situation. Also begin this exercise from varying positions or make it more difficult with a double wall pass.

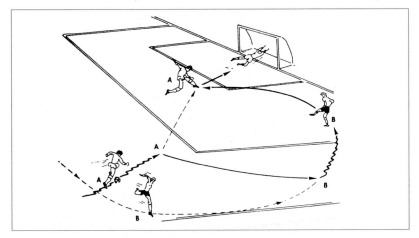

Exercise 8: In closing we can also have the players carry out a number of game situation moves, whereby the accent is on the goal shot. We can use numerous examples from the various training sessions. For example an exercise in which the goal shot must be carried out quickly and under difficult circumstances, such as in the return pass. The result often depends on the player who makes the last pass: low followed by a shot or high followed by a header. Always put all the energy into the closing action and go to every ball .

15 Post-season

A difficult season is over. The last games have been played and the time for a well-earned rest has come. Soon the players can devote themselves to the glorious vacation period with sun, food and doing nothing. The following weeks, above all the way the players spend their leisure time, will to a great degree influence the preparatory period of the next season. Relative rest does not mean that you eat until you are round. It would be just as senseless to carry out extremely hard individual training in order to be "top fit" at the first training. The objective is to relax in an active way. The batteries must be recharged. This is best done by forgetting soccer for a while and devoting your time to other sports which promote recovery. It is extremely important to never overdo it.

A negative example from my coaching experience was a very good defender who during his holidays went on a tour with a well-trained group of racing cyclists every day. The result was that he had to start the new training programme with tired muscles. Sports such as handball, volleyball, tennis and badminton, on the other hand, are very well suited. But there are many more possibilities. Try to develop new game forms at the beach. These could be games in which the (soccer) ball is the focal point if you can't live without a ball. Here are some examples:

Target ball: Stick a flagpole in the sand. Whoever hits the pole gets a point. Another attempt is allowed if you hit the opponent's ball.

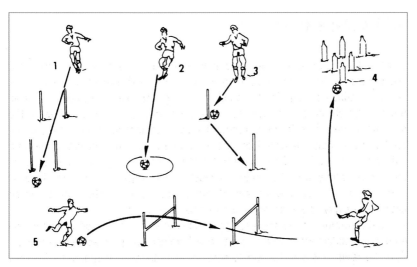

Soccer golf: Everyone knows mini-golf. Use a few simple aids, such as a flagpole, plastic bags filled with sand, to create various obstacles which must be overcome with the ball.

Examples:
1. From a distance of 5 to 10 m shoot the ball through a "goal" formed by two poles standing close to each other;
2. Play the ball into a marked circle with as few attempts as possible;
3. Play the ball against flagpoles in a predetermined sequence;
4. Knock over a number of plastic bottles filled with sand as skittles;
5. In one action shoot a ball over the first hurdle and under the second.

16 Postscript

This book was written to give coaches a lively and practical guide for structuring training. It does not profess to cover everything. The usually complicated theories about the game and training of soccer have consciously only been touched on very slightly. We have also purposely avoided classifying exercise series. Instead we chose a practical method of proceeding which begins with the first day of the preparatory period and chronologically develops training further.

Organising a diverse training right through the entire season is a difficult task for the coach. In addition, the programme must make sense with regard to the players, this means that training must take the physical, technical and tactical possibilities of the particular players into consideration. The method chosen up by us not only makes this book unique in its effectiveness, but also gives every coach a guideline for his everyday work which recurs weekly. It enables him - absolutely including his own personal views - to put together a completely "ready to use" annual programme with which to train his group of players. If, with the book as a solid foundation for an annual programme, we were able to give numerous coaches of all playing classes better knowledge with regard to sensible training and give them new ideas, then we have achieved our objective.

Modern soccer, playing without the ball, total soccer. These terms make clear how the game of soccer has changed in recent years. The condition of the players and the playing systems are focused on more and more. Improvisation and bad preparation can lead to problems in the team within a short time. This book gives the coach tools with which to train his players and prepare them for today's fast, energy-draining game. Weekly, very intensive use of this book would the greatest recognition.

The Author

17 Photo & Illustration Credits

Cover photo: adidas
Imaging and cover design: Birgit Engelen
Illustrations: Jozef Sneyers